Borrowed Spaces

Life between the cracks of modern Hong Kong

CHRISTOPHER DEWOLF

PENGUIN BOOKS

UK | USA | Canada | Ireland | Australia
India | New Zealand | South Africa | China

Penguin Books is part of the Penguin Random House group of companies whose addresses can be found at global.penguinrandomhouse.com.

Penguin Random House
PENGUIN BOOKS

First published by Penguin Group (Australia), 2017

1 3 5 7 9 10 8 6 4 2

Cover design by Di Suo © Penguin Group (Australia)
Text design by Steffan Leyshon-Jones © Penguin Group (Australia)
Printed and bound in Hong Kong by Printing Express

penguin.com.au

ISBN: 9780734310859

FSC
www.fsc.org
MIX
Paper from responsible sources
FSC™ C012285

To Laine, who made this all possible

Hawker stalls on Peel Street, Hong Kong

Preface

When I visit a new city, I don't go to museums; I look for markets.

The first time I went to London, my itinerary was set by Andrew Richard Kershman's brilliant *London Market Guide*, which details everything from the touristy Portobello Road antiques market to the olives and okra for sale on Ridley Road. When I went to New York, I spent hours wandering around Chinatown, slurping sweet *tofu fa* served by two chatty old ladies from a Rubbermaid container on the street.

I love the dynamic of these spaces. They teem with customers, merchants, street performers, beggars, delivery men who handle dollies and pushcarts the way chefs wield their knives. It's the 'ballet of the good city sidewalk', described by the great urbanist Jane Jacobs, unchoreographed yet ruled by a certain unspoken logic.[1] I grew up in a suburban city that felt maddeningly dull, stumbling forward in a cold stupor, never quite alive.

When I finally encountered the magic of the sidewalk ballet, I was transfixed.

Hong Kong was a revelation. When I first came to Hong Kong in 2005, I was drawn to the junk stalls of Pei Ho Street, the surplus clothing of Fa Yuen Street and the unfamiliar fruits and vegetables sold on Graham Street. I marvelled at the green market stalls with their threadbare awnings from which dozens of products dangled from hooks. What struck me most of all was the way the entire city seemed to mimic the street markets I had found elsewhere, an entire city as lively as Ridley Road. A canopy of signs stretched out over every road, enclosing them in cathedrals of commerce.

When I began to travel around the rest of Asia, I started seeing parallels between each place, and it dawned on me that what I have always found most interesting about cities was the way they self-organise. In Tokyo, tiny lanes thread between yakitori stalls with room for half a dozen people, and potted plants surround little houses – everything unplanned yet human-sized and comfortable. It reminded me of the narrow back alleys of Montreal, where I would come across weekend garage sales, bicycle workshops and bookstores housed in backyard sheds. In many cities, the best places are the ones that have been planned the least: the informal spaces, borrowed and altered from their official uses.

What makes Hong Kong special is how many of

these borrowed spaces exist within the rigid framework of concrete housing estates and skyscrapers that are decidedly not human-scaled. I began to realise that if you stripped away all its accoutrements – laundry hanging from bamboo rods, street market stalls, assertive neon signs, potted plants in the street, awnings and news-stands and red market lamps – Hong Kong would be little more than a barren landscape of ugly concrete buildings. It would be as cold and vacant as the suburbs I left behind.

And yet, that is exactly what is happening. Bit by bit, Hong Kong's informal spaces, its palimpsest streets that have accrued so many layers of life through the years, are being homogenised. The charm of Hong Kong is the way people have transformed this often hostile and inhuman city into something vibrant and liveable. But the balance is now tipping from the informal towards the tightly controlled – something I have been privy to as a journalist documenting these changes.

Hong Kong is in the midst of an existential crisis. Twenty years after the transfer of sovereignty from Britain to China, the city is stuck in a political quagmire between authoritarianism and liberal democracy. A new generation of Hong Kongers is questioning the fundamental values that underpin this place, casting a critical gaze on the establishment and its ambitions. At the same time, the city's urban fabric is being radically reshaped, with hawkers cleared off the streets and entire blocks of small buildings bulldozed to make way for new shopping malls and towers.

There is a strong connection between city's urban spaces and its cultural, social and economic well-being. A healthy city allows for a certain give and take between citizens, as well as between citizens and their government. Debate rages over whether Hong Kong will ever enjoy democracy in the sense of electing its own leaders, but true democracy has more to do with the everyday lives of citizens and their ability to shape the city around them. That's why any consideration of Hong Kong's future must include a dialogue about the health of its urban environment. This book is my modest contribution to that discussion.

Christopher DeWolf
Hong Kong
December 2016

Borrowed Spaces

I tried to keep up as we darted across a roundabout and traced our way down the curb of a highway interchange. The Mango King was waiting. 'We call him the Mango King because he loves mangoes so much,' explained my guide, Michael Leung.

Leung was born in London, and worked as an industrial designer before moving to Hong Kong, where he became a designer in the most conceptual sense of the word. 'Michael is about almost everything except the object,' Aric Chen, M+ Museum's design curator, once told me. 'He represents the generation of designers-as-activists who have pushed the role of the designer away from commerce and industry and towards social enterprise and grassroots organising. As a designer, he's 100 per cent locavore.'

I met Leung when he started installing beehives on rooftops in collaboration with a local beekeeper. These days, he helps run a market stall in Yau Ma Tei, where he trades in community interaction more than any material goods. When I walk with him through the neighbourhood, it seems like everyone knows him: the butcher, the greengrocer, the driver of the delivery van who slows down just long enough to shout a greeting. He must be the most popular man in Yau Ma Tei.

In a way, that's how he met the Mango King. In 2013, Leung was working on a project about community gardening when some friends introduced him to a man who had turned a patch of empty land in the middle of an interchange into a flourishing urban farm. A year later, he took me to see the farm. As we approached a hole in a chain-link fence, Leung ran through a partial list of the Mango King's bounty: one lychee tree, four banana trees, five mango trees, twenty cayenne chilli plants, forty papaya trees, 75 square metres of potatoes and an indeterminate number of pineapple trees.

We carefully passed through a hole in the fence and emerged into a clearing surrounded by horsetail trees, their long, spindly leaves fluttering in the wind. I looked around. A concrete flyover rose in the distance and the white noise of traffic filtered through the trees, but it was hard to see any passing cars. There was a small lean-to at one end of the site. Plastic jugs of water were lined up in the dirt. 'There's no running water here, so I fill them up at a shopping mall nearby,' explained the Mango King when he wandered over to greet us.

The Mango King is a short, sturdy man with a deep tan and the kind of taut, leathery skin that comes from spending most of your life outdoors. Earlier, Leung had asked me to buy some mangoes from the market, and I handed them to the Mango King, who thanked me and set them aside. He explained that, once he ate the fruit, he would plant the pit; this is how he grew some of his other mango trees. He pointed towards a group of tiny seedlings. 'Ten years – that's the fastest a mango tree will grow from seed, if you want mangoes,' he told us. Near the mango trees, a few pineapple heads stuck out of the ground, gifts from neighbours in Yau Ma Tei.

The Mango King talked enthusiastically about his produce, but he was cagey about his past. 'I think he's had a rough life,' Leung told me. At some point, the Mango King ended up homeless, but rather than sleep on the streets, he staked a claim to this piece of land and started growing food. 'Back in my village in China, I dabbled in farming with my friends – actually, it was more like I watched them grow things,' he said to us. 'Growing things, it's all about experience and how passionate you are. If you're not into it, nothing will grow.'

In a sense, the Mango King is a pioneer. The land we were standing on is man-made, 'reclaimed' from the sea in the early 1990s in order to build road and rail links to Hong Kong's new airport. Two decades later, it is a disjointed mess of roadways, isolated housing estates and ratty vacant lots. The Mango King is the first person to live on this patch of land and the first person to grow food from its soil. Legally speaking, though, he is an intruder. This is government land, which in Hong Kong means it is no man's land.

Leung told me that passing motorists sometimes call the police when they see the Mango King cooking dinner outside his shack, but the authorities generally tolerate his presence. Still, his future is never certain. 'I've only been doing this for a year here, but there's construction nearby and some surveyors told me they might kick me off this land,' said the Mango King. 'But that wouldn't be for at least half a year, and by then I'll be harvesting.'

One word to describe what the Mango King is doing is 'illegal'. Another word to describe it is 'informal'. From afar, Hong Kong appears to be a rigorously planned assembly of lookalike high-rises, glossy shopping malls and orderly roadways criss-crossed by footbridges – Fritz Lang's *Metropolis* come to life, a vertical city ruled by technocrats and industrialists. Look closer, however, and another city comes into focus: a city of makeshift market stalls and unauthorised neon signs, of citizen-built gathering spaces and illicit carts hawking curry fishballs.

This hidden unruliness comes with the territory. In 2009, a young French photographer named Romain Jacquet-Lagrèze moved to Hong Kong and became fascinated with the way nature asserts itself even in the harsh, denuded canyons of Hong Kong's concrete jungle. He eventually published a book, *Wild Concrete*, which documents the way nature reclaims the city. A seed dropped into a drain can give birth to a banyan tree that clings tenaciously to the side of an old concrete tenement building. The last time I met Jacquet-Lagrèze, he took out his phone and showed me a photo of a mysterious vine climbing up the side of a high-rise. 'I had no idea what this strange-looking plant was,' he said. He swiped right to another photo. A fuchsia fruit had begun growing from one of the vine's tentacles. 'It's a dragon fruit!' he exclaimed, marvelling at the image. Hong Kong is full of these surprising corners and unexpected wrinkles. It's a city with a lot to say.

That's especially true when it comes to Hong Kong's borrowed spaces – its street hawkers and squatter villages, its hidden artists' colonies and ephemeral bamboo theatres. These are part of what scholars call informal urbanism: the process of building a city outside of an official framework. It's a phenomenon that manifests itself in thousands of different ways in cities around the world. When an African immigrant in Paris lays out a blanket of knick-knacks in a *marché aux puces*, it's a contribution to the city's informal life. So are the jeepneys of Manila, cobbled together from old Army jeeps to fill the gaps left by public transport. Even food trucks in Los Angeles are part of the phenomenon, whether they offer fusion Korean tacos or traditional Filipino fare – they're the motorised descendants of street hawkers that have plied their trade for centuries.

In the most simplistic sense, informality is what happens when a city's formal framework fails to accommodate the full scope of urban life. But it's hard to draw a firm line between the two. 'The binaries of "informal" versus "formal" cannot be understood as absolutes,'[2] warned Christian Werthmann, a professor of landscape architecture at Leibniz University in Hannover. He noted that governments typically take a dim view of informality, but a growing number of academics, architects and citizens see it as an undervalued resource in a world that is quickly urbanising. 'The biggest lesson we can learn from informal space is of participation and collaboration. There's a certain social cohesion in informal spaces that you have a hard time finding in newly constructed neighbourhoods by the government or the private sector.'[3]

This dichotomy is also key to understanding an essential part of Hong Kong's character. It is a city that has been shaped by the tension between informality and attempts to control it. In the years following World War II and the Chinese civil war, hundreds of thousands of people moved from mainland China to Hong Kong, which was then a British colony. A decade after the war, Hong Kong's population had doubled to more than three million. There wasn't enough housing for the newcomers, so many built homes for themselves in shantytowns that rose on the hills above Kowloon and Hong Kong Island. At the same time, migrants made work for themselves by selling things on the street: cheap food for factory workers, fruits and vegetables, surplus stock from factories. This continued for nearly three decades after the war. By the 1970s, there were more than 50 000 hawkers in the streets. All of this existed outside the framework of the law; shantytowns were built illegally on government-owned land, and most hawkers operated without permits and without paying rent.

Such independent organisation has happened in hundreds of cities around the world, but Hong Kong's unique geography and history gave it an added twist. Hong Kong is a city *in extremis*, caught between mountains and water, with complicated land policies that have created one of the most densely populated urban centres on earth. There are many competing demands for a very limited amount of space. The government's response is to exert increasingly tight control over how that space is used, so there is constant tension between public behaviour and the restrictions to which it is subjected.

In many ways, that's what defines Hong Kong's urban form. This is a city of identikit buildings built to the maximum of what current building codes allow, blank slates that are shaped by their inhabitants according to need, like a banyan tree growing out of a stone wall whose roots eventually subsume its inorganic surroundings. You can see examples of this all over the city, where perfunctory concrete apartment blocks sprout illegal additions meant to expand living space. Illegally-built houses are common on rooftops, for example, clustering together to form villages that resemble the shantytowns once found on Hong Kong's hillsides. Given the three-year waiting list for public housing, demand for these rooftop huts is as high as ever.

The same appropriation of space occurs at street level. Public space in Hong Kong is inflexibly designed, with fences and walls that restrict movement and outdoor furniture that is uncomfortable and unattractive. People respond by putting their own tables and chairs in the street. The same thing happens on undeveloped hillsides around the city. On a hill near Mong Kok, people have used concrete and kitchen tiles to make benches; bamboo to make railings, which could then help them up the steep slopes; and tree branches to hang exercise equipment. Chinese altars were built in the woods using styrofoam boxes and discarded pieces of cardboard. Now, the sound of Cantonese opera and the clatter of mah-jong tiles float through the woods.

There's a sharp contrast between these informal spaces and the hierarchies imposed by centralised development. You can see this in the government's urban renewal projects, which replace street markets and small-scale housing with shopping malls and high-rises, and it's even clearer in the steep 'ladder street' staircases of Central and Sheung Wan. The elderly have typically responded to these slopes by trimming the legs of household chairs and placing them at intervals on the steps, so that they can rest while climbing uphill. The formal response is to build escalators, which facilitate movement uphill and – not coincidentally – boost property value and development potential of the hillside streets.

In 1975, just as Hong Kong was beginning to impose strict controls over urban space, Michel Foucault published *Discipline and Punish*, which evoked the concept of the panopticon to describe the systems of social control to which we are subjected. What interested another French intellectual, Michel de Certeau, was how that control is subverted in everyday life. Here's what he wrote in response to Foucault:

> If it is true that the grid of 'discipline' is everywhere becoming clearer and more extensive, it is all the more urgent to discover how an entire society resists being reduced to it, what popular procedures (. . .) manipulate the mechanisms of discipline and conform to them only in order to evade them.[4]

How does this manifest itself in Hong Kong? Urban designer Michael Siu calls it 'guerilla wars in everyday public spaces'.[5] It's an apt metaphor. Every winter, merchants in the Mong Kok flower market gear up for Chinese New Year by loading up on orchids, orange trees and other traditional New Year plants. The market is patrolled by hawker control officers from the Food and Environmental Hygiene Department (FEHD), who unofficially allow the merchants to use a small amount of public space to display their extra wares; if the officers decide that goods obstruct public passage, they can impose hefty fines on the merchants. Every year, there are arguments between officers and merchants, who argue that the officers' decisions are arbitrary and unfair. Many hawkers have complained to me that officers on different shifts give them different and sometimes contradictory instructions. In 2015, the Legislative Council's parliamentary subcommittee on street hawkers raised a red flag about this behaviour: '[The] FEHD has been issuing summons to hawkers quite frequently that seems to aim at eradicating them,' it noted in a report.[6]

This kind of conflict can be seen on an even larger scale in Tin Shui Wai, a master-planned New Town built in the 1980s. In order to build the town, the Hong Kong government had to buy land from Cheung Kong Holdings, the city's biggest property developer, which insisted on a secret deal – exposed only in 2010 – that gave it a virtual monopoly on the town's retail spaces. As a result, food prices in Tin Shui Wai are some of the highest in Hong Kong, even though its inhabitants earn less than those in any other city district. For many, the only affordable option is to shop at the early-morning 'dawn market', a gathering of illegal hawkers. Crackdowns on the market by hawker control officers have sometimes been deadly; in 2008, a hawker was running away from the officers when he fell into a nearby river and drowned. Similar illegal markets exist in poor neighbourhoods all over Hong Kong – the roots of public needs and desires wrapping themselves around the hard surface of urban space.

All cities have informal life; all cities attempt to control it. This relationship can be productive, as officialdom learns from the successes of informality while reigning in its excesses. But in Hong Kong the relationship has become toxic. Even worse, the situation is compounded by the city's ongoing identity crisis. Trapped between questions of language, culture and politics, the day-to-day life of the city risks being overlooked. Twenty years after its handover to China, Hong Kong is once again in a state of existential angst, and the struggle for its soul is being waged not only in the classroom, courtroom and boardroom, but in the streets.

Flouting the Law Since 1842

On a muggy summer afternoon, I met up with Michael Leung at Kai Fong Pai Dong, a hawker stall on Hamilton Street that he opened in 2015. It's meant to be a kind of community space, where neighbours can sell second-hand goods and sit down for a chat. The name translates to 'Neighbours' Stall'. Running this kind of stall on Hong Kong streets means subjecting yourself to a byzantine array of rules and regulations. 'I've kind of realised that we break the law every day when we open here, not only because of what we sell but the space we occupy,' he told me. 'In Hong Kong, there's so many rules, it's easy to break them. Some of the rules are ridiculous.'

We'll get into those rules in a moment. But first, it's worth noting that Leung's observation is hardly unique – not to him and not to hawkers of this era. Hong Kong became a British crown colony in 1842, a year after the British won the First Opium War, and the colony quickly became a trading hub that drew thousands of migrants from mainland China. Many of them made a living by selling food and dry goods on the street. The first attempts to control hawkers came in 1872, when the government passed an ordinance issuing wooden permits that needed to be renewed four times a year, at a cost of fifty cents. The same ordinance also banned hawkers from calling out to advertise their wares in Central and on the waterfront.

Their shouts filled the air in other parts of the city, however. By the middle of 1873, there were 1146 licensed hawkers and 'about as many' others who operated illegally, according to a letter written by the Reverend J. Nacken, a British missionary living in Hong Kong. The letter was rediscovered in 1968 and published in the *Journal of the Royal Asiatic Society*.[7] Nacken estimated that if every hawker cried out once per minute for seven hours a day, there were at least 1 million cries uttered every day. 'That may seem an extravagant calculation on my part; but if someone will stand for ten minutes on any spot in the busy parts of the Chinese quarter and count the street-criers who pass by, he will doubtless become inclined to agree with the above estimate,' he wrote.

Nacken made detailed notes of each kind of hawker. 'The Chinese generally are early risers,' he noted, 'but the congee hawker has been up an hour or two before sunrise.' He described how hawkers carried their rice porridge in two boxes hanging from a pole over their shoulders, each containing a pot heated by a small fire. 'As they pass your door you have your choice,' wrote Nacken. 'You may have pigs' blood congee, fish congee, mulberry-root flavoured congee, or barley, or kidney or pork and a variety of other congees.'

After the congee hawkers came the vegetable vendors, offering celery, watercress and spinach in the spring, pumpkins and eggplants in the summer, caraway plants, taro and cabbages in the autumn, and mustard greens, garlic and parsley in the winter – among many other varieties of produce. Fish and meat hawkers emerged later in the day, offering fresh pork and *haam jyu*, Cantonese salted fish. Nacken wrote that minced-meat hawkers in Canton (present-day Guangzhou) advertised their wares with the help of a display case decorated with 'licentious' images – pornography, in other words, which was not tolerated by Hong Kong police.

Illegal hawkers have always played a cat-and-mouse game with police, much to the chagrin of Hong Kong residents, who enjoy the hawkers' presence. In May 1931, an article in the *China Mail* described the case of an Indian police sergeant who arrested two hawkers for selling slippers without a license. 'A crowd of Chinese coolies collected and began to abuse the Sergeant,'[8] reported the newspaper. One of the labourers grabbed the policeman by the belt and shoved him forward, causing his turban to fall off. Though the labourer was hauled away and charged with assault, he filed his own charge of assault against the sergeant, which was eventually dismissed by a judge, who described him as 'a very saucy man'[9].

Hawkers gained the upper hand after World War II, when hundreds of thousands of people poured into Hong Kong from mainland China, escaping the instability of the civil war between the Nationalists and Communists. Streets were teeming with hawkers and outdoor restaurants known as *dai pai dong* – literally 'big license stalls' – because their oversized permits were displayed prominently above their outdoor kitchens. (Today, the term *dai pai dong* refers only to those stalls allowed to serve cooked food.) Each stall had its specialty: wonton noodles, beef balls, roast goose, coffee and tea. When shops closed for the day, the spaces in front of their metal shutters filled with tables and chairs. Many *dai pai dong* were open late, their woks roaring until two or three o'clock in the morning.

One Yau Ma Tei café owner, Yeung Hon-yuen, spent his childhood in the *dai pai dong* his family opened in 1955, when he was five years old. He started doing odd jobs for his parents the following year. By the time he was fifteen, his family's business had grown to three stalls, so he quit school to work in the stall on

Canton Road, where he sold milk tea, coffee, toast and sandwiches. The foods were high-calorie, localised versions of Western dishes that were meant to fill the bellies of hungry shift workers.

'We had nine or ten tables,' he recalled,[10] though the exact number of tables depended on how many customers there were and whether police were on patrol. Though the stall was legal and licensed, they weren't permitted to put tables and chairs out on the street. Yeung kept the stall open from 6:30 a.m. to 5:30 p.m. every day except for the three first days of the Chinese New Year. Like many *dai pai dong* owners, he often slept on a wooden plank in the stall in order to guard against thieves.

Hong Kong was a rough and tumble place back then. The influx of mainland refugees fuelled an industrial boom, but it also strained the city's ability to govern itself. Corruption was rampant. Police would order food from the stalls and have it delivered to the station – without paying a cent. The police were bullies, but they weren't as dangerous as the triad gangs that ran illegal brothels, gambling dens and loan shark operations. They preyed on most businesses by demanding protection money.

Despite these hardships, life in the streets was exciting. Night markets became known as 'poor man's nightclubs'. For working-class families, these informal activities were an affordable source of nourishment and entertainment. On Temple Street, you could get your teeth pulled, watch a snake dance or have your fortune told by a bird. Space in the market was entirely unregulated, but gentlemen's agreements ensured that hawkers occupied the same spot every night. In 1959, a century-old night market moved from the streets of Sai Ying Pun to a waterfront car park in Sheung Wan, where it became known as the Dai Daat Dei – literally 'Big Open Space'. Every night, an estimated 3000 people thronged the lanes between bamboo-frame stalls selling sundry goods before settling down for a midnight feast of wok-fried prawns and clams in black bean sauce.

Hawkers didn't rely on banks for their financing. Instead, they made use of informal networks known as chit funds. Every month, a group of hawkers would get together and elect a leader to manage their savings, which created a pool of money that each member of the group could tap into. Many of the *dai pai dong* owners were from the Chaoshan region of eastern Guangdong province, which is known for its braised meats, gregarious culture and the expression '*ga gi nang*' – 'our people'. For Chinese immigrants such as these, the streets offered a chance to build a new community in an alien place.

A similar kind of self-organisation occurred when Hong Kong descended into the turmoil of 1967. There was widespread dissatisfaction at the time with rampant corruption and poor working conditions; these frustrations eventually erupted into a series of labour disputes. These were exploited by Communist sympathisers, who hoped to bring China's Cultural Revolution to Hong Kong in order to overthrow the colonial British regime. When bus drivers went on strike, jitneys that operated in the rural New Territories began illegally picking up customers in the urban areas of Kowloon and Hong Kong Island. Rather than ban the new service, the government made it official, licensing the jitneys as 'public light buses' and allowing them to operate routes throughout the city. In the midst of strikes, riots and general upheaval, the government felt it was better to embrace the jitneys – or at least tolerate – than it was to suppress them.

Dai pai dong, street markets and minibuses are just a few of the informal – and either currently or previously illegal – systems that shaped Hong Kong into the city it is today. Although people have lived in Hong Kong for thousands of years, it was the post-war influx of refugees and their borrowed urban spaces that created the cultural, social and economic geography of modern Hong Kong. It was in the *dai pai dong* that the city's famous 'soy sauce Western' cuisine of milk tea, fried egg sandwiches and macaroni noodle soup was born. Street markets continue to provide fresh groceries for a large number of Hong Kongers; various studies estimate that just under 30 per cent of the population buy their groceries primarily from traditional wet markets.[11]

*

The post-war boom also turned Hong Kong into a truly vertical city. As housing development and public facilities struggled to keep up with demand, people began to colonise rooftops, turning them into outdoor schools, chicken coops and places to kick around a soccer ball. They built houses, too. If someone saw that a rooftop hut had been erected on the building next door, they would add one to their own property in order to earn a bit of extra cash. In the working-class neighbourhoods of Kowloon, there were rooftop huts as far as the eye could see.

My father-in-law, retired architect Alfred Tam, grew up in one of those huts, sharing the space with his mother, two brothers and sister. 'The hut we lived in was built of brick, 10 by 10 feet, with a covered space of 10 by 15 feet annexed to it,' he recalled with an architect's precision. Theirs was the only hut to begin with, but they were eventually joined by another family – relatives of the landlady, who built a slightly larger hut on the opposite end of the roof. 'There was ample open space between us,' he recalled. 'In fact, the rooftops of all the buildings on the street were interconnected. To us, it was a vast playground.'

All of this was in response to a built environment that served only the most basic needs. After World War II, there wasn't nearly enough housing for the thousands of refugees pouring across the border, so most of them built shacks on the steep slopes surrounding Hong Kong's urban areas, replicating the rural villages they left behind. Sin Sin Man, an artist and designer, grew up in a squatter village in Diamond Hill. Her walk home from school took her past shacks of varying quality, vegetable fields, a distillery making the pungent herbal liquor *ng ka pei*, malodorous pig farms and the main hall of a Taoist temple, which was always filled with incense smoke.[12] 'I saw and smelled a zillion things every day,' she told me.

This experience stood in contrast to the increasingly rigid way the formal city was being developed. An architect once remarked to me that Hong Kong doesn't have architecture; it has building typologies. Because land here is so scarce and so valuable, and because everyone builds to the maximum dimensions of what building codes allow, buildings in Hong Kong tend to be replicas of one another. Before World War II, there was the shophouse, a kind of structure built by Chinese people across Southeast Asia that combined a ground floor shop with upper-floor residences. This morphed into the more modern *tong lau* after the war, which themselves grew into enormous, mixed-use structures known as composite buildings, featuring apartments, small factories, restaurants and other businesses side by side. After that, codes restricted mixed-use structures, mandating taller, skinnier towers so that more natural light and ventilation would reach the streets.

At the same time, Hong Kong's government was quickly building public housing for people displaced by the fires that frequently tore through the wood shacks of squatter villages. These early public housing estates were utilitarian to the extreme, with simple 9.3-square-metre units shared by multi-generation families. The tiny apartments had communal washrooms and outdoor corridors that doubled as shared kitchens. Bare concrete tarmacs stood between the blocks. Though amenities improved with successive generations of public housing, they retained the basic concept of densely packed housing blocks with empty space in between. This was even replicated by private developments like Mei Foo Estate, a behemoth of ninety-nine blocks that opened in 1966 as Hong Kong's first private housing estate. Public housing in Hong Kong was designed to shelter as many people as possible for as little money as possible. Private developers added another goal to the equation: extract as much profit as possible.

Even private housing provided only the most rudimentary outline of accommodation, leaving residents to fill in the blanks. *Dai pai dong* and hawkers set up shop in public housing estates, stringing their vinyl awnings between lampposts. Rooftop villages sprouted on top of housing blocks. Apartment-dwellers extended their living space by erecting cages around their windows, which they then filled with potted plants and wet laundry. Because apartment buildings were and are so dense, people don't have common space. Your living room is the street; your dining room is the restaurant downstairs.

This situation creates a rich and dynamic street life, but it also creates a management problem. For years, activity in the streets of Hong Kong was only loosely regulated, but by the 1970s, the government decided it was time to assert more control. The theory at the time was that, as cities transitioned from 'third world' to 'first world', such informal uses of urban space would dwindle as the economy developed and people became wealthier.[13] Hawkers were an extension of the industrial economy, providing low-cost food and goods to the working class, who could take advantage of the savings this provided to accumulate capital and work their way up the socioeconomic ladder. One day, the reasoning went, there would no longer be any need for hawkers, *dai pai dong*, squatter villages or anything of the sort.

In light of this argument, the Hong Kong government opted for a policy of elimination through attrition. Squatter villages were frozen in place, their residents prohibited from expanding their homes until they could be replaced with public housing estates. Street hawkers were licensed and regulated. In some cases, hawkers were given fixed pitches in busy street markets, allowing them to continue selling affordable fruits and vegetables to the neighbourhoods that needed them. In other cases, hawkers were relocated to designated areas, which they developed, bit by bit, into informal marketplaces using do-it-yourself roofing, electrical wiring and even plumbing. Still more were forced to move into dank, windowless concrete marketplaces, away from streets that were filled with an ever-growing number of cars.

The catch was that, while hawkers were still allowed to ply their trade, their licenses were made exceptionally hard to transfer. Even today, when a licensed hawker dies, his or her license can only be transferred to a surviving spouse. The intent was to eventually eliminate all street hawker stalls, and this 1970s-era policy is now well on its way to achieving that goal. In 2015, there were just 6133 licensed hawkers in Hong Kong; another 1440 work illegally. No new *dai pai dong* licenses have been issued since 1956, and the government has actively bought back licenses since 1983. Today, only twenty-five *dai pai dong* remain in the city, compared to around 3000 in the 1950s.[14]

Where the government's policy failed was in assuming that the need for hawkers and informal housing would eventually abate. Hong Kong's transition to a service economy, along with economic competition from mainland China, has undermined the social mobility that characterised Hong Kong in the 1970s and '80s. If it was ever easy to pull yourself up by your own bootstraps, that is no longer the case. The poor remain poor; the rich grow richer. The city's Gini index, which measures income inequality, rose from 45 in 1981 to 54 in 2011, by far the highest level among economically developed countries. Since 1995, the percentage of Hong Kong people living in poverty has grown from 14.8 per cent to 18 per cent.

There's a widespread sense that something has been lost as the fabric of old Hong Kong becomes worn and thin. Australian-born actor and Cantonese pop singer Gregory Rivers – better known by his Chinese name, Ho Kwok-wing – summed up the sentiment in a 2016 interview with the *South China Morning Post*, reminiscing about freshly fried *yau ja gwai, or* savoury doughnuts, which he used to buy from stalls on the street.[15] For Rivers, the disappearance of those doughnut stalls is symptomatic of Hong Kong's greater deterioration. 'Thirty years ago, people in Hong Kong were extremely happy,' he said. 'They knew that if they worked hard, they would be able to secure a future. But today everything is so expensive . . . For most people, even if you worked extremely hard, you can't save enough for even the down payment on a new apartment.'

The crackdown on informal life isn't necessarily responsible for the persistent inequality and decline of social mobility in Hong Kong, but there's a case to be made that it has exacerbated the situation by denying people access to affordable products and the ability to become entrepreneurs. It has made the city less dynamic and interesting. I think it has made it less happy, too.

In 2016, the United Nations-backed World Happiness Report ranked Hong Kong as one of the least happy countries in the world.[16] Researchers at the University of Hong Kong have found a link between happiness and built environment: people who live in extremely regimented urban environments are measurably less happy than those who live in places with better public space.[17] By killing the life in its streets, Hong Kong is slowly killing itself.

Twilight City

The gunshots woke me just after 2 a.m. I wasn't sure what they were at first, but it was an unnerving sound. I made my way into the living room and turned on the TV to see footage of a wide-eyed policeman pointing his revolver towards a crowd, then raising it into the air and firing twice. It was an astounding sight. Guns are rare in Hong Kong, and while most police officers have them, I had never before seen an officer draw his or her weapon. All of this for a few carts selling fishballs?, I thought.

Earlier that evening, I was on Portland Street, a few blocks away from my home, eyeing a squid being engulfed by the flames of a charcoal grill. It was 8 February 2016, the first day of the Chinese New Year, a time when hawker control officers traditionally take a few days off and let the streets return to how they were decades ago. People wheeled carnival games onto the sidewalks of Argyle Street and set up barbecues on the pavement near my apartment. Hawkers sold fishballs and charcoal-fired egg waffles to hungry, nostalgic Hong Kongers.

But this time was different. The atmosphere was tense. A year earlier, in 2015, New Year hawkers had been chased from the streets of Sham Shui Po by hawker control officers. They made their way to a busy stretch of Portland Street in Mong Kok, where they were guarded by young activists from the localist movement, which had recently emerged to counter the influence of mainland China in Hong Kong. Now the hawkers were back on Portland Street, where they set up their stalls beneath the looming stone exterior of Langham Place, a shopping mall and office tower built on the site of a former bird market.

Almost immediately, officers forced them off the main street and into narrow alleyways. Then the localists came. They escorted the hawkers back onto Portland Street, arguing with the hawker control officers, who called the police for help. When the police arrived, they came with helmets, riot shields and snarling dogs. Surreally, hawkers continued selling their dishes, indifferent to the powder keg behind them. At that point, abandoning the squid, I made my way to the sidelines, ceding ground to reporters who were dressed as if venturing into a war zone.

The real violence started after I had returned home.

Police began chasing away protesters, who retaliated by throwing bottles and bricks torn up from the street. Some police officers threw bricks back into the crowd. People on social media began calling it the Fishball Revolution. Police battled with protesters until ten o'clock the next morning, when things finally calmed down. Later that day, I walked through Mong Kok on sidewalks liberated of their bricks.

Some editorialists claimed that protesters had used the informal night market as an excuse to attack the police, but this argument ignores the role of street hawking in the local democracy movement. Shortly after the first Chinese New Year confrontation between hawkers and police, I met up with Kel Lee, a recent university graduate and member of Hong Kong Indigenous, one of the upstart localist groups that emerged during the pro-democracy Umbrella Movement, which occupied the streets of Admiralty, Mong Kok and Causeway Bay for seventy-nine days in 2014. Sipping locally brewed beers at a Mong Kok bar, Lee told me he saw hawkers as an intrinsic part of Hong Kong's entrepreneurial culture. 'If you work hard, you'll have the opportunity to move up, and hawker culture is part of that spirit,' he explained.

Lee said that many of the New Year hawkers were young people who hoped to earn a bit of extra cash during the holiday, since wages for university grads have been the same – about HK$10 000 or HK$12 000 a month – for many years. A cart costs less than HK$10 000, so they sell fishballs during New Year to earn money. Hong Kong Indigenous not only protects the hawkers from hawker control officers and the police, they also help clean up when the night market is over. 'The government tries to say the hawkers are dirty, but we showed they aren't,' Lee said. 'The environmental issues can be managed.'

Food hawkers aren't the only ones targeted. Every evening around Kweilin Street in Sham Shui Po, after the licensed street markets selling second-hand electronics, fabric and assorted knick-knacks close for the day, a second wave of hawkers arrives to set up an illicit night market. They spread out blankets on the pavement and cover them with old vinyl records, used household appliances, old shoes, bicycles, Chinese god figures – a hodgepodge of items that would otherwise end up in one of Hong Kong's overburdened landfills. The market takes place for two hours each night, when hawker control officers open an unofficial window for hawkers to sell their wares. Recently, though, there have been more and more instances where officers prevent the night market from opening at all. When the officers arrive, several hawkers shout *yau gwai* – 'Ghosts!' – which some say is a holdover from the days when most hawker control officers were non-Chinese known colloquially as *gwai lo*: ghost men.

Even licensed businesses are affected. In the north-eastern corner of Mong Kok, there is a century-old flower market that once consisted entirely of informal hawkers. After the government restricted the size of the area in which they could ply their trade, they migrated into shopfront commercial spaces in the 1980s. Though originally wholesalers, much of their business now depends on retail customers, especially around Chinese New Year, when it's tradition to buy orchids, kumquat trees and other auspicious plants. The shops display flowers and plants in the streets, infusing the neighbourhood with a sweet fragrance – and irritating the hawker control officers, who are in constant battle with the merchants.

'We were the first to put our plants out in the streets, before there were so many other flower shops. Now everyone does it,' said Cheung Yuk-hing, who ran an alleyway flower stall for more than thirty years. I first met him in 2009, when I lived down the street, and he complained bitterly that hawker control officers seemed to favour some businesses over others. 'We've followed them to the other flower shops and they don't do anything to them,' added his daughter, Kelly Cheung, who started helping out at the stall when she was six years old. Each ticket costs thousands of dollars, and the Cheungs had already been fined six times in the past week, she complained at the time. I recently walked past their stall, curious to see how things were going. It was gone.

Things vanish suddenly in Hong Kong; it's part of the rhythm of life in such a restless city. But the informal aspects of city life are especially vulnerable to disappearance. Around the time I came into contact with Cheung Yuk-hing, I began meeting people who live in rooftop villages just like the one in which my father-in-law was raised. The difference is it's now sixty years later and roof-dwellers are much less likely to become architects, doctors and business people. Today, most of the escape routes from poverty have been sealed off. The government estimates that more than 1200 rooftop huts remain in Hong Kong's urban core. From my balcony in Mong Kok, I can spot more than a dozen such houses, including one that was built less than a year ago.

Rooftop settlements are often described as slums, and in many respects they are. Families crowd into single rooms, roofs leak, pests are common. And yet they have a dignity that is missing from the squalid subdivided flats that have become common in recent years. On a sweltering afternoon in the summer of 2009, I climbed ten floors to the top of a building in Tai Kok Tsui that was slated for redevelopment. I was surprised at how peaceful it was. Rows of houses were lined up against utility pipes, which served as access corridors that occasionally widened into clearings filled with drying clothes. Potted plants sighed in the heavy heat of summer. Door gods peeled from wooden entryways. The city's noises receded into the distance, replaced by birdsong and the buzzing of cicadas. It felt almost like the countryside.

A friendly social worker, Phoebe Lo, was helping the rooftop's 100 residents find new places to live, and she introduced me to several of them. The first person we met was Yu Wing-hong, a handyman who told us he had lived on the roof for thirty years. He first arrived to house-sit for a friend who left for mainland China. 'He never came back, so I stayed,' Yu shrugged. He started making small improvements to his hut. In an empty space where the building's staircase meets the roof, he built a bathroom out of sheet metal. Next door, he built a compact kitchen with a gas stove and refrigerator. From there, a steep wooden staircase led to a cockloft with a living room and an air-conditioned bedroom. It was an impressive construction, and Yu seemed proud of his work. He told us he had applied for public housing years ago, and been given the option of an apartment in one of three faraway suburbs. He ultimately decided he wanted to stay in Tai Kok Tsui – his home turf, where he had friends, neighbours and the feeling of home.

Around the corner from Yu's place, I met the Yim family. Born in Hong Kong, Mr Yim had spent much of his life working as a cook in Bangkok, where he met his

Thai wife. They had two children. In 2007, the family moved to Hong Kong and Yim bought a two-bedroom rooftop house 'for a small amount' from his brother. The house was tidy, with new appliances, a desktop computer and a large fish tank in the living room. An air conditioner hummed as we spoke. 'I know these structures are illegal, and if we have to move out, we will,' he said. He worried that the rooftop was vulnerable to burglars, and it might be hard to escape if there was a fire. 'But the neighbours here are close, and everyone knows each other,' he told us. Yim, too, had applied for public housing. He said he hoped he would still be able to live nearby, close to his children's school, though in all likelihood they would be offered a flat somewhere on the city's outskirts.

In a typical Hong Kong apartment building, neighbours barely know each other. But on the roof, residents wandered around in slippers and pyjamas, hanging up laundry and sharing gossip. One evening, a few weeks after my first visit to the roof, I returned to meet Sam Fong, a 23-year-old university student who shared a hut with his parents and sister. Compared to his neighbours, he was more philosophical about life on the roof. He described how his family hosted an annual feast for Mid-Autumn Festival in the open space in front of their hut. 'We live with our neighbours rather than just living next to them,' he said. 'When it's raining, my mom will step outside and yell, "*Sau saam lah*" – "It's raining!" – like in a village. We depend on each other.'

Fong invited me into his living room. A large flat-screen television was mounted incongruously next to a wooden ladder that led up to the cockloft where his entire family slept. 'It's very warm, sharing such a small space with your family,' Fong said. Born and raised in Guangzhou, Fong moved to the roof two years ago to join the rest of his family, who had already immigrated to Hong Kong. His father worked as a security guard, his mother as a waitress and his sister in a clothing store. When he wasn't studying, he worked part-time at a supermarket.

Fong didn't know where his family would go when the building was torn down. Because none of them were permanent residents, they weren't eligible for public housing, and the rooftop hut was all they could afford. Fong had started working at the supermarket to help contribute. 'At least we're together,' he mused. 'So many new immigrants are like us, but since we have no political voice or power, we have no choice but to accept our situation. All we can do is to be here for each other.'

Over the years, I visited dozens of rooftops around Hong Kong. In Tai Kok Tsui, I met a Pakistan-born security guard who had applied for public housing and was hoping to bring his wife and daughter to Hong Kong. In Kwun Tong, I met the Cheungs, a couple in their eighties who were the last remaining residents in a cluster of huts that once housed several families; they told me how Typhoon York had ripped the tin roof off their house in 1999. In Sham Shui Po, I paid a visit to Shane, an East African who had escaped torture in his home country and was applying for asylum from the local UN office – a notoriously long and difficult process. He wasn't allowed to work, so he spent much of his time on the roof, drinking beer and surveying the city.

There is a grey market for rooftop houses: places to live that are bought, sold and rented under the table. In 2009, a 28-square-metre rooftop hut could sell for as little as HK$40 000 – less than 5 per cent of what an equivalent apartment cost at the time. Renters get less value: a 2013 government study reported that the median rent for a rooftop hut was HK$2200 per month. The catch, of course, is that rooftop huts are illegal, and if they are cleared for redevelopment, owners are not necessarily entitled to compensation.

More often than not, I had a sense of déjà-vu when I visited a new rooftop. I eventually realised it was because I had already seen them depicted in *Portraits from Above*, a 2009 book by Rufina Wu and Stefan Canham that documents five rooftops through photography and precise architectural drawings. 'People are very ingenious and very resourceful designers. They can make use of every inch as capacity. I find that fascinating,' said Wu when I reached her by phone in

Vancouver. I asked if she ever revisited the rooftops she documented. 'As far as I know, four of them are demolished already,' she said. 'The book very quickly became a historical document, which is kind of strange. We kept in touch with a couple of residents but it's very difficult – we don't have their phone numbers anymore, some of their emails are not in use anymore. Now that the building is gone, it's difficult to keep track of everyone.'

There was an initial surge of demolitions in the early 2000s when the government cleared rooftop huts from buildings with only one staircase. The real estate boom that followed the global financial crisis took its toll, too, as hundreds of old buildings were bought up and redeveloped. Recently, though, things seem to have settled down. If the government wanted to, it could clear away all the rooftop houses in a year or two. But that would exacerbate an already dire housing crisis, so the government turns a blind eye to the rooftop huts that remain – and the illegal real estate market that supports them. The number of rooftop houses hasn't changed much in recent years, but more families than ever are squeezing into them. A hut that was once home to a single person might now accommodate an entire family.

Given the long wait for public housing, and the fact that people have lived affordably in rooftop houses for decades, why can't they simply be legalised? The government could send inspectors to make sure they are structurally sound, and offer low-interest loans to fix huts that need repairs. Hong Kong's rooftop villages are basically aerial shantytowns. In cities around the world, from Medellín to Rio de Janeiro, these kinds of informal settlements have been successfully retrofitted, giving their inhabitants a chance to improve their situation without uprooting their lives. But that may just be a fantasy. Hong Kong's government seems unlikely to ever adopt such an unorthodox solution to the housing problem. The city's political paralysis and increasingly rigid bureaucracy seems to have sapped whatever creative energy it once had. Nobody wants to take responsibility if a radical new solution doesn't work.

Like Wu, I have lost touch with most of the rooftop villagers I met. Sam Fong gave me his phone number and email address, but both seem to have stopped working long ago. 'They've moved already,' said Phoebe Lo the last time I called her. 'Some of them rented flats nearby. Some got public housing already. Some of them stayed with friends.' Compensation ranged from HK$10 000 to more than HK$100 000 per household, paid by the holding company that bought the building on behalf of a large property developer. Shortly after my last visit, two mysterious fires broke out in the building. Some residents suggested that the holding company had set the fires to drive out the rooftop dwellers, but nothing came of those accusations.

Today, a collection of upmarket high-rises are under construction on the site of the old walk-up building and its rooftop village. The hoardings announce a new lifestyle destination called Square Mile, developed by Henderson Land, one of Hong Kong's large property conglomerates. 'The developer has started to approach potential tenants, mostly chain eateries,' reported a construction industry newspaper in 2015. Low-rent rooftop huts and hawker stalls are not part of the plan, presumably.

*

There's an expression that was common before the handover: 'Hong Kong is a borrowed place on borrowed time.' These days, that saying has been supplanted by a single word: twilight. There is a pervasive fear that everything distinct about Hong Kong is vanishing in the face of globalisation and integration with mainland China: the Cantonese language, greasy-spoon *cha chaan teng* diners, even the common law legal system. 'This is a twilight industry' is a refrain commonly heard from red minibus drivers, bamboo craftsmen and everyone in between.

In the case of neon signs, it is a literal twilight. The lambent glow that once bathed Hong Kong's streets is quickly fading. Streets that were recently festooned with giant neon emblems have been cleared of their signage in a remarkably swift government effort to crack down on signs exceeding building regulations. This despite the fact that, in many cases, signs were erected legally in the 1970s and '80s, a time when there were few limits on what shop owners could install on the façades of their buildings. That has led to the disappearance of many iconic signs – giant illuminated fish, naughty strip club signs, elegantly rendered Chinese characters and more. 'People still have this image in their minds of Hong Kong as a city filled with neon signs, but if you look around now, there are actually very few of them left,' said Aric Chen, who oversees the design and architecture programme at M+ Museum.

Sammy's Kitchen is a prime example. For nearly four decades, a giant neon cow marked a curve in Queen's Road West as it entered the Hong Kong neighbourhood of Sai Ying Pun. *Sammy's Kitchen Ltd.*, it read in jaunty italics. The eatery was one of the first in Hong Kong to transplant the Chinese-Western fusion cuisine of *dai pai dong* to a formal restaurant setting. The sign quickly became a landmark: 'Take me to the cow!' became a familiar refrain for Hong Kong taxi drivers.

The restaurant was opened in 1969 by Sammy Yip, who had worked in hotel restaurants and wanted to bring more affordable Western classics to a working-class neighbourhood. In 1978, he spent HK$30 000 – about the price of a flat – to commission a 3-metre-long, 2.4-metre-tall signboard that projected halfway out into the street. Sammy's daughter Iry grew up with the cow. For thirty-two years, the sign existed without causing trouble, casting a red and green glow on the street below. Then, in the spring of 2010, the Buildings Department ordered its removal, claiming that the building was too old. 'It's sixty years old,' Iry acknowledged at the time. 'But our cow was always well maintained. So many other signs were never maintained, so we thought, Why does this one have to be removed?'

The family decided to fight the removal order, but by 2012 they had exhausted all avenues of appeal. 'My dad doesn't like trouble, so he said, "Okay lah, better move on,"' recalled Iry. That's when an American journalist who lived near Sammy's Kitchen, Doug Meigs, contacted M+ and asked if they had thought about collecting the sign. The museum got in touch with the restaurant, which agreed to donate the sign if the museum arranged its removal. That launched a whole additional round of bureaucratic tussling. Despite the Building Department's insistence that the sign be taken down, it took more than two years to arrange all the necessary approvals, as M+ negotiated with various government agencies to temporarily close the street so a crane could remove the neon cow.

'Hong Kong has this reputation of being free market and laissez-faire, but it's actually a highly bureaucratic and technocratic city,' said Chen. Instead of adopting a case-by-case approach that could have allowed Sammy's to keep its sign in place, Chen said the government has a top-down mentality and a one-size-fits-all approach to policy. That stands in contrast to the way Hong Kong was managed in the past, when there was a certain allowance for informality. The clampdown on street hawkers, rooftop huts, window cages and signboards are all part of the same shift in attitude that has occurred over the past two decades.

In 2014, Chen put together an online exhibition, NeonSigns.HK, which included a documentary on the city's dwindling tribe of neon craftspeople and essays on the history and legacy of neon signs. But the renewed focus hasn't done anything to halt neon's disappearance. If anything, it has accelerated, but M+ has collected just four neon signs. Chen told me it can be hard to anticipate when a sign will be removed, and even when they catch one before it gets taken down, business owners are often reluctant to donate. Sammy's cow now sits in storage as M+ builds a permanent home, which is slated to open in 2019.

Recently, a wave of business owners have commissioned new neon signs to give a touch of Hong Kong flavour to their bars, restaurants and cafés, but these efforts are modest. Times have changed; a typical retail lease runs for just two years, which is far too short to justify spending hundreds of thousands of dollars on a handmade neon sign. Of course, some of the old signs have been allowed to stay. As long as it is no more than 4 metres in length, a sign can be granted approval. The only problem is that business owners must hire a government-approved contractor to inspect the sign and recommend improvements. It is often cheaper to have it removed than to get the required approvals.

The result is a quiet transformation of Hong Kong's streets – one that has happened so quickly, many have yet to notice. Tiffany Tang, who works for the heritage conservation group Urban Discovery, explained that she was in the midst of taking photos of the few signs that remain on Tai Nan Street in Sham Shui Po, where a dwindling number of building supply shops advertise their goods with red Chinese characters on white signboards – one character per board, arranged in a neat row that extends into the middle of the street. Compared to the cacophony of neon on other streets, these workshop signs were insistent yet polite.

Now they are mostly gone. As Tang took photos, a shop owner asked what she was doing. 'I told him the signs aren't there anymore, and then he looked up and yes, "Oh yes, they are gone!"' she said. 'Then he added, "Okay lah, they are useless anyway."' Tang threw up her hands in exasperation. 'It's so heartbreaking to hear that they don't even care. It's intangible cultural heritage. It's not just a sign – it's part of what Hong Kong means.'

Later, I spoke with Kevin Mak, an architect who has documented the signs on Instagram, where he has a large following. 'For me, the cultural value lost by taking down old signage is the same as taking down a heritage building,' he said. Since his grandmother never went to school, he explained, her reading material was limited to what she saw in the streets on her way to work. 'She learnt to read and write Chinese by studying signboards,' he said.

The signs are even more important to Hong Kong's identity than most of its buildings. Whether you are in Ngau Tau Kok or North Point, most buildings look the same; what distinguishes each neighbourhood is the detritus of human activity that accumulates on buildings like barnacles on the hull of a ship. Signs embody the competitive entrepreneurial character that made Hong Kong famous. Their arrangement is informal and seemingly ad hoc, but there is an underlying logic to it, as each sign jockeys for the best and most visible position. Without its signs, Hong Kong loses the three-dimensional character that makes it distinct from every other city.

*

Signs aren't the only things that give Hong Kong's urban fabric its unique texture. Every city has its own material language, and Hong Kong's consists of vinyl tarps,

Sammy's Kitchen neon sign in 2011, before it was removed

Hawker stalls on Tai Yuen Street in Wan Chai

repurposed sheet metal and deceptively strong rods of bamboo. You can see this in the bazaars that emerged when the government set aside vacant land for hawkers to settle in the 1970s. One such bazaar, on Yen Chow Street in Sham Shui Po, specialises in surplus textiles from garment factories. It's known primarily by its nickname, Pang Jai, which roughly means 'Little Temporary Place'. Over the years, the bazaar has become a warren of stalls filled with bolts of fabric in every colour and pattern imaginable. Vinyl tarps shelter hawkers from the elements, and the bazaar is lit by fluorescent lights held up with ribbon. A few large trees grow in the midst of this organised chaos.

You can guess what happened next. In 2015, the government announced that Pang Jai would be redeveloped into housing, and began negotiating with the hawkers. In early 2016, curator Mary Lee staged a mini-festival to underline the importance of Pang Jai to people like fashion designers, who love the bazaar for its factory rejects that can't be found anywhere else. 'It's not just about the hawkers – there's a broader cultural issue,' she said. 'The government's plans are top-down instead of bottom-up and naturally developed. If things continue like this, there will be no more hawkers in Hong Kong. It will become a very boring city.'

The innovative, improvisational spirit that built Pang Jai extends even to the seemingly immutable shells of concrete that fill Hong Kong's many industrial areas. Blocks built in the 1970s to house garment factories and warehouses are now home to art galleries, music venues and studios where designers and artists both work and live – all of which fall into a legal grey area, since the buildings are still zoned exclusively for manufacturing and warehouse use. A pillar of Hong Kong's independent music scene, Hidden Agenda, has had to move five times because the government keeps shutting it down for running an entertainment venue in an industrial block, yet there is no way for it to apply to operate legally. Renting space in a commercial block would be prohibitively expensive; several live music venues have shut down in recent years because of exorbitant rents.

Rules are useful and necessary; it's a good idea to prevent industrial spaces from being filled with wood subdivisions that block fire escapes, for instance. But they become oppressive when the hand that applies them is too heavy. By contrast, a light touch can produce unexpectedly happy results, which is what happened in 1998 when the government let artists use one of its buildings with few restrictions. After the property market crashed due to the Asian financial crisis, the government suspended all sales of its own property. One of the sites saved from the chopping block was the Oil Street Government Supplies Depot, a vast warehouse in North Point. Space inside the building was rented out for an affordable HK$2.50 per square foot, which drew the attention of artists, architects and designers, who moved there en masse.

By the end of 1999, it had become a thriving creative village, the likes of which Hong Kong had never seen. People whose only experience of culture had been stuffy government venues now plunged into Oil Street's exuberant atmosphere with giddy enthusiasm. There were impromptu performances, celebrity photoshoots, rooftop DJ sessions. People now speak about Oil Street in reverential tones.

A few years ago, I was having a drink with Rupert Wong, the owner of Sense 99, a kind of quasi-legal bar that operates in an old Central shophouse. He pulled out a stack of photos taken in the Oil Street warehouse in 1999, describing impromptu performances and wild exhibitions. There was a general sense of camaraderie and creative fervour. 'And there was a bar,' he grinned, pointing to the well-stocked shelves of liquor. In the photo, an old television sat on one end of the bar; it lives on at Sense, where it now functions as a fish tank.

Oil Street was shut down when all its tenants were evicted in 1999. The government planned to sell the site, but it ended up sitting vacant for more than a decade before it was sold for redevelopment into a hotel. Wong has tried to keep a part of the Oil Street ethos alive at Sense. 'It has a very natural, self-regulating atmosphere. It feels like it has no rules, but everybody gets each other,' he told me.

In an even broader sense, Oil Street's legacy survives in other creative spaces that have emerged throughout the city. But they risk following the same path as their predecessor. In 2016, a deadly fire in an industrial building that had been illegally subdivided into storage units prompted the government to crack down on the unapproved use of industrial blocks. By the end of the year, it had cleared out seven buildings, forcing the closure of a theatre, gyms, yoga centres, restaurants and a Taoist shrine. When I contacted the Lands Department to find out how far the government planned to go, I received a vague answer from a spokesperson: 'It depends on the actual operation of the particular use and the relevant lease conditions of the lot.' In other words, the government may decide to wipe out all the creative endeavours happening in Hong Kong's industrial buildings. Or it may not. If the government has a plan, it isn't saying.

This kind of thing mirrors what people from all walks of Hong Kong life have criticised. Faced with the complicated task of managing a big, diverse city, the government has done away with any allowances for improvisation or flexibility and relied on a rigidly prescriptive set of rules. I was curious to find out how this came to be, so on a sunny day in October, as a dry autumn breeze pushed back the thick heat of summer, I made my way to the forty-first floor of a government office tower in Wan Chai. That's where I met Kim Salkeld, the head of the Efficiency Unit, which is tasked with improving collaboration between government departments and making them more transparent to the public.

If there's anyone who can speak with authority about the inner workings of the government, it's Salkeld, who first joined the civil service in 1980. His first job was in the New Territories Services Department, which dealt with public space on the city's suburban fringe. Before he was transferred to the Efficiency Unit, he worked for half a dozen government departments, from Social Services to the Central Policy Unit, and he was Deputy Secretary for the Environment in the late 1990s.

'Any large organisation has patterns of doing things,' he explained, sipping from a mug of warm water. Salkeld has wire-rimmed glasses and a boyish haircut that belies his fifty-seven years. When he speaks, it is softly, his words chosen carefully. 'You have to have a constant process of examining whether people at the front line are listening, and whether they are empowered, enabled and encouraged to adapt and change the way they react – or are they told, "These are the guidelines, you must follow them."' That kind of constant re-evaluation is not happening in Hong Kong, according to Salkeld. 'The civil service has traditionally been quite guideline-dependant.

You have a lot of traditions and assumptions coming out of the UK that aren't indigenous. If you don't understand why the rules and regulations are the way they are, it's difficult to exercise initiative.'

To make matters worse, there has been constant pressure over the years to do more with less, despite Hong Kong's ample wealth. Even as the government's fiscal reserves hit an astonishing HK$859 billion in 2016, public hospitals were starved of cash, pensioners made do with paltry payouts and there was a four-year waiting list for public housing. A lot of this has to do with pressure from the private sector to keep the low-tax, laissez-faire policies so praised by neoliberal economists like Milton Friedman.

'The accountants have had much more influence than the political leaders,' noted Salkeld. His voice lowered and he seemed to choose his words with particular care. 'There was always a tension on the money side. In most areas of expenditure, the pattern in Hong Kong is, it's not simply a matter of the civil service mentality. It's the very strong influence of businessmen who think that any cost is wasted. The old colonial approach was you wanted to commit to as little recurrent expenditure as possible, to keep taxes as low as possible so you reduce political problems.'

What Friedman never realised on his fly-by visits is that Hong Kong is no free market paradise. The government's lack of oversight has allowed monopolies and cartels to dominate the economy, while an overburdened civil service has been starved of the resources it needs to look laterally at Hong Kong's problems. 'What I've observed over the past twenty years is increasing reliance on the guidelines because you really don't have time to do anything else,' Salkeld said. 'The frustration is not just among the population trying to interact with the government, it's also among frontline civil servants.'

Penny-pinching isn't the only reason for the government's calcification. Hong Kong is a strange sort of hybrid state, halfway between a city and a country. The chief executive of Hong Kong has wider-ranging responsibilities than the mayors of London or New York – everything from immigration policy to the homeless in Kwun Tong. Things get lost in between. In other large cities like London or Tokyo, many things that directly affect citizens are dealt with by local borough councils, but the closest equivalent in Hong Kong, district councils, are advisory bodies with no legislative power. This seems unlikely to change anytime soon, as Hong Kong's rulers in Beijing are afraid that more autonomous and influential district councils would be dominated by anti-establishment politicians.

There's a cultural dimension to the problem, too. 'Hong Kong is a fairly conservative place generally,' said

Salkeld. Many Hong Kongers are naturally risk-averse. At the same time, they are fiercely critical when something goes wrong. Salkeld pointed to the Planning Department's push to pedestrianise streets in Hong Kong's busiest neighbourhoods in the early 2000s. Some of the new pedestrian streets were victims of their own success, like Sai Yeung Choi Street in Mong Kok, which was filled to overcapacity with commercial touts that blocked the way and street musicians whose late-night performances drew noise complaints from nearby residents. Eventually, the local district council pressured the government to allow cars back onto the street.

'We didn't understand enough and didn't invest enough in engagement with the local community,' said Salkeld. 'Too often, we've rushed out and tried to be good guys, but if it doesn't work, the people at the top say, "Well, this failed," and people get discouraged.'

The Efficiency Unit tries to avoid that kind of outcome by implementing design labs for different governments to test new ideas on a controlled basis. Some of the ongoing projects include helping the public library system deal with the growing number of people who use libraries as social spaces without borrowing books. The unit has also established 1823, a platform for citizens to report anything from overflowing rubbish bins to illegal parking. Employees of 1823 redirect complaints to relevant departments and keep tabs on whether the issues are solved.

Despite these projects, Salkeld seems to recognise that he is fighting an uphill battle. That's especially true given that Hong Kong is caught in a political deadlock over questions of democracy. In 2014, two months before the Umbrella Movement exploded onto the city's streets, district councillor and urban planning activist Paul Zimmerman wrote in the *South China Morning Post* that Hong Kong needs more than a chief executive – it needs a mayor.

'The exhausting distraction of constitutional and political arrangements continues to divert much energy from our senior leadership, and has done so ever since [the handover negotiations began in] 1982,'[18] he wrote. 'This diversion is the reason why many government departments are operating under outdated practices, guidelines and statutes, unable to get the support they need from the top for making changes, as well as the cross-bureau and cross-department coordination that such changes involve. One solution suggested by many is a division of labour between the chief executive and the chief secretary, not unlike the roles of party secretary and mayor we see in mainland cities.'[19]

It's not a bad idea. And it echoes many of the things that Salkeld told me in his office. 'Politics is the art of living together in a city,' he said before we parted ways.

'You can do it well or you can do it badly.' If Hong Kong doesn't want to fade into the night, it needs somebody willing to negotiate the gap between the city that exists on paper and the city that exists in reality.

Build Your Own City

Walking through Hong Kong raises my blood pressure. I'm a dedicated pedestrian; given the choice, I prefer to walk. Considering that less than 10 per cent of Hong Kong's population get around by car, you would think I'd be in good company, yet the streets here are anything but pedestrian-friendly. There are few trees and even fewer benches. Roadside fences pen you into narrow, overcrowded sidewalks, lest you dash into the street and get in the way of the Toyota Alphard minivans beloved by the chauffeured class. There are plenty of small parks, plazas and 'sitting-out areas' – a quaintly named variety of gated public space that usually consists of a few benches and some shrubs – but many of them are poorly designed. One sitting-out area on Queen's Road East consists of two benches and a patch of concrete surrounded by a wall.

On paper, Hong Kong has a lot of public open spaces, but they aren't quality spaces. You get the sense that most of the city's public outdoor areas exist to tick boxes on somebody's checklist; they aren't designed for people to actually gather and chat, or lie down for a quick lunchtime nap. If you aren't sitting rigidly on a bench, staring straight ahead, these spaces aren't for you.

Serbian architect Selena Savic calls this kind of thing 'unpleasant design'. In an interview with the *South China Morning Post*, she said it 'refers to things that are intentionally and successfully rendered unusable, or uncomfortable for people to use. It's not about objects that are badly designed, but the opposite – objects, devices and spaces that are well designed in order to prohibit a particular use or behaviour'.[20] In other words, it's a form of social control. Design a bad bench so homeless people don't linger; fence off your sitting-out area so people don't spend too much time there.

In more suburban places, this hostile architecture has contributed to a decline of the commons, as more and more people spend their time in private spaces. But Hong Kongers don't have that kind of luxury; they need an outlet from their tiny apartments. So they make their own space.

In a quiet alleyway behind Hollywood Road, a group of old men gather around folding tables to play cards and Chinese chess. Listening to the radio – Cantonese opera on weekdays, horse races on Sunday – they sit on threadbare office recliners, second-hand stools, worn wooden dining chairs. At night, the wail of opera gives way to boozy laughter as this makeshift living room is taken over by patrons from Club 71, an adjacent bar named for the annual pro-democracy march. It's time-shared urban space.

This isn't anything deliberate; the people who use these borrowed spaces don't pay them much thought. It's just a pragmatic response to an uncomfortable urban environment. In Hong Kong, the line between public and private space has always been blurry. Shops spill onto the streets like overflowing Aladdin's caves. Someone places an altar beneath a tree and it grows into a neighbourhood shrine. In Tai Hang, a teenager put a shrine to the earth god beneath a banyan tree. People from the neighbourhood added their own god statues and Buddha figures. Now, seventy-odd years later, that teenager is a 90-year-old man who lives in the makeshift temple with a black mutt.

Something similar has happened on Duckling Hill, an undeveloped hillside in the suburban New Town of Tseung Kwan O. When people began moving into the area's housing estates in the 1980s and '90s, they discovered that there was a glorious view of the sea from the summit of Duckling Hill, but the hill's thick vegetation proved hard to penetrate. The only way to get to the top was by using a rope strung precariously between posts. So one day, a man decided to build some stairs.

He and a friend who worked in construction salvaged iron bars and mixed some concrete. They made the steps one by one. It took a day to make each step and 150 days to finish the staircase. Eventually, people took notice and began making contributions of their own. Some rescued plants from the garbage and used them to plant a garden, complete with a rainwater irrigation system. Others built pavilions with bamboo rods left over from a construction site, stocking the structures with household furniture and homey touches like clocks and calendars. Now it's a place made by the people, for the people.

The crowdsourced facilities on Duckling Hill differ from those built by the government in a number of ways. The hand-built pavilions provide better shelter from the rain and wind than the concrete shelters built by the government, which were designed according to a template and without consideration for the hill's specific weather conditions. Whereas the government installed benches facing a walking path, Duckling Hill walkers placed two benches together, set back from the path, oriented to take advantage of the view. Friends walking up the hill sit on the benches while they chat and look out to sea.

As inventive as they were, the Duckling Hill interventions were not welcomed by the government, which periodically tore up the gardens and knocked down the shelters. By 2006, park-goers were fed up with the constant tug of war, and they petitioned the government not to demolish their structures. Their pleas fell on deaf ears. In 2011, when the government planned another clearance operation, the people of Duckling Hill launched another petition, this time collecting 1036 signatures. They also drew the attention of two social workers who began liaising with the government. Around the same time, two researchers from the Polytechnic University of Hong Kong, Geraldine Borio and Caroline Wuethrich, stepped in to offer a design workshop that led the government to reconsider its stance.

This wasn't the researchers' first foray into Hong Kong's informal spaces. 'We came to Hong Kong with the intuition that there was something interesting going on,' said Borio when I met her for coffee near her office. Previously, they had been examining the way people in Bangkok appropriate the empty space beneath elevated highways. 'It's how people deal with the space under a lot of constraints that is interesting,' explained Borio. 'It's in these informal spaces that you find the most creative aspects of the city, because everything else is standardised. Hong Kong public spaces are very regulated, but in a back lane or on a hillside, you can do whatever you want.'

In Hong Kong's alleyways, I have seen restaurant workers washing dishes, nightclub staff burning offerings to the gods and Filipinos singing karaoke at folding tables. There are barbers and shops selling mah-jong tiles. In one Mong Kok alley, street sweepers have built an outdoor living room, complete with a daybed and an altar to the gods. In another alley near Gough Street, there is a small mirror screwed into the wall. I always wondered why it was there until I saw a man stop in front of it, inspect his reflection and pull out a comb to fix his hair.

All of this activity takes place within the remarkable constraints of Hong Kong's extreme density. Because spaces are so tight, a single object or installation rarely has just one function. Hong Kong's newsstands are a prime example. In 2015, Rufina Wu – the architect who documented Hong Kong's rooftop huts – turned her attention to the sidewalk kiosks selling magazines, newspapers and sundry goods. 'Every Sunday, my family would go for dim sum together in the morning, and we would typically find two or three newsstands on either side of the Chinese restaurant,' she told me. 'That would be when my brother and I would be allowed to pick up comic books on the way to dim sum.' A few years ago, she noticed that there seemed to be fewer newsstands than she remembered, which piqued her interest. She began drawing newsstands and talking to their owners. Her partner, Stefan Canham, took long-exposure photographs that captured each newsstand's role as an anchor in the fast-moving current of the street.

What struck Wu immediately was the newsstands' variety. Most consist of a cupboard and a shelf protected by an awning, but there are endless variations on that basic formula. 'Every single one of them is unique,' she said. 'Cities like London and Paris have their [standardised] newspaper kiosks and those are very iconic and emblematic of the city – you see them from a distance and recognise them. In Hong Kong, all of them are kind of camouflaged. Each location has its own specificity that it needs to respond to.' In other words, the location governs what products are sold. If a newsstand is near a school, there are toys that catch the eyes of passing children; newsstands in Central stock lots of English periodicals; in Tsim Sha Tsui and Causeway Bay, political books banned in China draw the attention of mainland tourists. 'Not many people notice these things,' said Wu. They take it for granted and keep on walking.

The one unifying element of the newsstands is their ability to transform. Newsstands that sprawl onto the sidewalk during the day must be closed up tight at night, which means retractable shelves and cubby holes for magazines. There is a certain amount of flexibility built in to all the structures, as newsstands are creatures of the street – expanding and contracting with the passing of time, negotiating with their surroundings in order to peacefully co-exist. It's the kind of thing that makes cities such interesting places.

The architectural vocabulary of jury-rigged hawker stalls, newsstands and *dai pai dong* has begun to coalesce into a local design language. Over the past couple of years, two young architects, Aron Tsang and Roselia Leung, have begun designing tables and chairs that hang on Hong Kong's ubiquitous roadside fences. 'It was a response to what the government has been doing, like spending hundreds of thousands of dollars on kiosks that don't protect anyone from the sun or rain,' said Tsang when I met him and Leung at a festival on Des Voeux Road Central, where they were displaying some of their work. Tsang gestured to a table mounted on the fence nearby. The fence is inert, yet with a table installed on its top, it suddenly comes alive with potential.

I looked around. Children were playing on the pavement next to us, but they were penned in by a temporary fence and two rows of fluorescent orange pylons, which separated people from the trams that were slowly rumbling by. Although the festival was part of a campaign to promote the idea that Des Voeux, a perennially congested and polluted street, should be dedicated to pedestrians and trams, the government had insisted on the extra barriers at the last minute. It felt more like a festival for traffic cones than for the public. Tsang shook his head. 'It's typical over-management,' he said. In some corner of the government's offices, a bureaucrat had a terrifying vision of pedestrians running amok. And so we were penned in like animals.

A block away, the festival's organisers had strung up a poster that asked whether the tram tracks should be fenced off when the street is pedestrianised. People were invited to put a sticker under their preference. Opinion was split pretty much down the middle. 'It's a cultural mindset. A lot of Hong Kong people stick to the rules,' said Leung. 'Hong Kong traditionally has a mixed culture – you see street markets everywhere, but the attitude of the government is to manage everything strictly, so they've created more and more rules as to how you can use the space.'

*

Hong Kong has a split personality, one side at war with the other. The Umbrella Movement made this division very clear. For seventy-nine days in 2014, thousands of people camped out in the streets of Admiralty, Causeway Bay and Mong Kok, protesting the restrictions Beijing had placed on the universal suffrage promised by Hong Kong's Basic Law. As the days went by and protests morphed into tent cities, it was as if Hong Kong's subconscious had bubbled up to the surface. People used to rushing through the streets were confronted with the opportunity to linger and think about their surroundings. They lay down. They made art. They rearranged highway lanes into little living rooms. The city's *genius loci* – its very essence – was on display.

Occupy, as the encampments were known, borrowed its name from Occupy Central, a campaign of civil disobedience that had been promised for a year if Beijing and Hong Kong leadership reneged on their pledge to reform Hong Kong's electoral system. That campaign was meant to be a tightly organised takeover of the central business district by 10 000 protesters, but what actually erupted in 2014 was something much larger and more spontaneous. When police deployed tear gas on student protesters on 28 September, hundreds of thousands of ordinary people took to the streets in solidarity. Because Hong Kong has no grand civic space that unites the people, they made their way to the exhaust-choked thoroughfares that dominate the urban landscape.

Occupy was not just a protest for democracy – it was an exercise in democratic place-making. In some way, big or small, it offered an answer to everything that is wrong with Hong Kong's urban environment. Air pollution declined by 80 per cent in Admiralty after cars were banished from the roads.[21] Freed from traffic, the streets filled with masses who quickly developed into a community; even anti-Occupy people had a corner in Mong Kok where they gathered and swapped conspiracy theories about CIA involvement in the protest. In Admiralty, concrete walls were covered with posters and sticky notes, and an entire roadside planter full of bushes was replaced by an organic farm growing seasonal vegetables. For anyone who had ever dreamed of a friendlier, more equitable Hong Kong, Occupy was a kind of paradise.

A few weeks after the occupation began, I found myself standing on what was normally an eight-lane funnel of angry traffic in Admiralty. The only sounds I could hear were footsteps and the soft murmur of voices. Free of diesel exhaust, the briny scent of the harbour lingered in the air, and a warm breeze ruffled the nylon shells of tents laid out in tidy rows. Walking along the flyover, my back towards the heart of the encampment, I passed beneath a canopy of umbrellas, knit together and strung between foot-bridges to shade the street below. Nearby, a handful of men stood measuring plywood, cutting it into furniture to make this inhospitable roadway more comfortable. They had already turned old shipping pallets and plastic crates into little staircases that helped people climb over the metre-high barriers that divided lanes of traffic.

I made my way over a barrier, walking towards the Lennon Wall – a curved concrete staircase named unofficially after the peacenik singer – that had become the focal point for the occupied zone. The wall and stairs were festooned with multicoloured sticky notes inscribed with messages. Some were vindictive ('689 is no fucking use,' one read, referring to Chief Executive CY Leung, who was elected by a total of 689 votes), but most were aspirational:

I trust in the people of Hong Kong!

If not us, then who? If not now, then when?

Dad, mum & those who are against us: I hope you will be with us and support us one day . . . We want true democracy only.

Rounding the corner, I approached the main entrance to the Legislative Council, where a library had emerged in the sheltered area next to the driveway. Protesters called it Democracy University, and it was filled with treatises on politics and society. It occurred to me that I rarely saw anyone reading a book in Hong Kong, yet Occupy was filled with readers, sprawled on the asphalt or perched on highway barriers, necks craned forward in the sodium glow of street lights.

The atmosphere at Mong Kok was different. Admiralty's car-oriented road network had created a cloistered village, but Mong Kok's dense grid of streets made the occupied area along Nathan Road more permeable, inviting passersby to mingle and gawk at the political banners. Every night, there was a nervous energy as people engaged in heated debates that sometimes turned into shouting matches. Admiralty felt insular, filled with middle-class students and office workers; Mong Kok felt vital. Near the southern end of the site, a group of Catholics built a shrine that came to be known as St. Francis' Chapel on the Street. A few metres away stood an altar for Kwan Yu, the Chinese god of war, which drew bowing worshippers to burn fresh incense throughout the day.

Hong Kong was alive in a way it hadn't been since I moved here in 2008. I felt I needed to contribute something. When I found out that Michael Leung and some friends had strung up a tarp on Nathan Road to make space for a library, I messaged him and asked if they had any use for my old grey sofa. They did. For weeks after, I passed by the nascent library and watched people sit on the sofa, reading books. People often used it to nap. Soon it was joined by another couch. Every day, the number of bookshelves around those couches multiplied. It was if we had planted a seed that grew into a garden, asphalt crumbling away under the pressure of new life.

There was a debate as to whether Occupy should be called a movement or a revolution; the term 'Umbrella Revolution' came first, coined by a Twitter user named Adam Cotton, who used it to describe the way protesters used umbrellas to shield themselves from police tear gas. Many felt it was too aggressive, so Umbrella Movement became the more politically correct term. But in many ways, the original name was more accurate, because what happened in 2014 was a revolution in the way people saw themselves and their city. For most of its history, Hong Kong was a place to pass through on the way to a better life. Now it is a place to stay.

After initial attempts to clear the occupied zones by force resulted in failure, the government relied on a number of third parties, including bus and taxi companies, to file suit against the protesters in court, claiming the road closures had affected their business. By the time the courts had issued an injunction, many protesters were too tired to continue their resistance. Mong Kok was cleared on 25 and 26 November; as the police sprayed protesters with liquid tear gas, one activist reportedly knelt before the St. Francis Chapel, performed the sign of the cross and sprinted away with the crucifix. Admiralty was cleared on 11 December and Causeway Bay four days later.

The clearance had an air of vengefulness about it. Banners were destroyed, libraries demolished. The farm that had been planted at Admiralty was uprooted; a few days later, the government's secretary for security, Lai Tung-kwok, fumed in the Legislative Council that protesters had 'turned over the soil in roadside planters for planting', seemingly unaware of the irony of his complaint.[22] If Occupy could be seen as form of place-making, then its clearance was the attempted elimination of place. Once the tents and posters had been cleared away, Harcourt Road was once again a funnel for traffic and nothing more. In the days after the clearance, I began to see Hong Kong's polluted, traffic-clogged streets as a form of social repression. Free thought cannot survive in a city of dead spaces.

But Hong Kong is not dead yet. The geography of the Umbrella Movement has survived, revealing itself in unexpected ways. The movement's spirit lives on, too. In recent years – and especially since Occupy – a new generation of activists has harnessed the city's informal life as a tool for civic empowerment. It was a year after Occupy when Michael Leung got a hawker license and began operating Kai Fong Pai Dong on Hamilton Street, in large part so the Mango King would have a place to sell his produce. Around the same time, an illustrator who goes by Flyingpig got in touch with Leung and asked if there was anywhere in the neighbourhood she could draw portraits of neighbours. Then a banana farmer named Tam Chi-kit was looking for a place to sell his bananas. The stall started with those three founders. Within a year, fifteen people were involved.

Leung said he came up with the idea for the stall while working on a variety of projects: visiting the Mango King, growing food on the rooftops of Yau Ma Tei, helping to run a pop-up flea market on the sidewalks of Shanghai Street. 'It's a platform for everything I've been working on for the past six years,' he told me one afternoon as we stood next to the stall. 'There are a lot of factors that have contributed to the decay of community in Hong Kong. Bad urban planning, shopping malls, high rents. Capitalism. It sounds grim, but it's actually a very gradual process. You see a local shop that sells drinks and snacks has closed down, another shop has become an estate agent.' The stall is an antidote to all of that, a community hub where neighbours can sell various goods, do creative things or simply hang out and chat.

Basically, Kai Fong Pai Dong articulates the true value of a market stall. Beyond the material goods they sell, the little booths in the street are tools of social cohesion. In many neighbourhoods, they are the most stable businesses around, chugging away even as the family-owned shops around them are replaced by impersonal chain stores whose profits flow directly into the coffers of multinational corporations.[23] They are reliable landmarks in a city whose pace of change can be alienating and disorienting.

There are forty-three so-called 'fixed-pitch hawker areas' around Hong Kong – otherwise known as street markets – home to 6300 hawker stalls. The biggest markets are thriving, including the always busy meat, seafood, fruit and vegetable stalls around Nelson Street and Canton Road, but many of the secondary markets are withering away – not for lack of business, but because the government is actively relocating stalls and buying back hawker licenses in order to clear the streets. The market around Kai Fong Pai Dong is one example. Bit by bit, over the years, its stalls have gone missing like teeth. You pass by a stall selling local eggs, another selling flowers, and then suddenly there is a two-stall gap. Between 2013 and 2015, a total of 481 hawkers surrendered their licenses.

There is a silver lining, however. Though the government is buying back licenses, it is also giving hawkers up to HK$54 000 to rebuild their stalls. This initiative goes back to a deadly inferno on Fa Yuen Street in 2011, when shoddy wiring caused an electrical fire that killed nine people. The fire spread to an adjacent tenement, which had been illegally subdivided into tiny cubicle flats with no fire escapes. Rather than cracking down on subdivided flats – Hong Kong's landlords are a powerful lobby – the government declared war on street markets. Hawker control officers immediately ordered hawkers to reduce their stock and scale back their stalls, removing awnings that protected them from the rain. 'It's like they wanted to blame everything on us,' said a hawker who sells children's clothing on Fa Yuen Street.

That's when a group of designers and community activists got involved, forming an organisation called the Street Design Union, which liaised between hawkers and the government. The most productive outcome of the project was something called Hawker Reload, a special metal market stall designed in collaboration with hawkers themselves. 'We visited 235 stalls and did visual surveys,' said Manfred Yuen, an architect who helped lead the project. At the time, there were just two kinds of official booths, one for wet goods like fresh food and another for dry goods like clothing. But hawkers had modified the booths to suit their needs. Yuen and his team recorded eleven different typologies. These studies resulted in a prototype with a retractable sheet-metal awning, to eliminate the need for flammable tarps. It also featured a system of movable carts and folding trays that make it easier to close up shop at night, when stalls are required to occupy no more than 1.1 square metres.

By the end of 2016, the government had received 2406 applications from hawkers who wanted to rebuild their stalls. Yuen said he took pains to ensure that the prototype could be easily adapted by individual hawkers. You can already see the effects of the scheme across Hong Kong, as battered wooden booths are replaced by new metal structures. Interestingly, most of the old booths were painted the same shade of dark green, but the new stalls are a rainbow of cheerful colours – pink, teal, lime green – as if to symbolise the spirit of renewal.

The renovation of hawker stalls is just one sign that official attitudes are changing. In 2015, the Legislative Council's subcommittee on hawker policy issued a report that echoed many of the things activists and hawkers have been saying for years. The report acknowledged the cultural and economic importance of hawkers, as well as the damaging effect the government's policy has had on them – and, by extension, on the vitality of Hong Kong as a whole. It concluded that the government should 'revamp hawker policy by a sea change in its approach' asserting the economic necessity of hawkers in a high-rent city and the 'place-making' dimension of hawking that creates lively, pedestrian-friendly streets.

The report contained a number of specific recommendations, including the establishment of new hawker bazaars and night markets that would be tailored to different districts. It suggested that the FEHD's monopoly on dealing with hawkers be replaced by a 'cross-bureaux/departments working group' that would take a holistic view of street hawking, hopefully ending the antagonistic relationship between hawkers and the government. Most importantly, it recommended making it possible for stall owners to pass their licenses on to employees. That measure alone would put an end to the forty-year war against Hong Kong's informal street life.

Of course, the report's recommendations are just that – recommendations. Whether the government will implement them is hard to say. 'I do not think this is high up on the administration's agenda,' said Alan Leong, a former legislator who was the subcommittee's deputy chairman. When I reached him by phone a year after the report's release, Leong – a barrister with a stentorian voice and a posh Oxbridge accent – told me that the secretary for Food and Health, a surgeon named Ko Wing-man, had seemed receptive to the subcommittee's recommendations. 'But the thing is, hawker policy in Hong Kong really is not only within the policy remit of Dr Ko,' he said. It spans town planning, commerce and transport. A true reform of hawker policy would require effort from several of the government's many branches.

The government's response to points raised by the report are catalogued in one of its appendices. 'The Government keeps an open mind' is a phrase used on multiple occasions – a sign of hedging more than anything else. Leong did note one interesting commitment, though: to give individual districts a chance to formulate their own hawker policy from the ground up. 'They expect initiatives to come from the localities where people would want to have implemented a hawker policy of one sort or another,' he said. Many people in Hong Kong are concerned that skyrocketing rents have made daily necessities unaffordable, so there is public pressure to ease pressure on hawkers. It's possible that, with enough public pressure, individual district councils could lean on the government to liberalise hawker policy in their districts.

Another member of the subcommittee, pro-democracy legislator Claudia Mo, said she was sceptical that any meaningful change would occur. In November 2016, the government said it could allow a temporary Chinese New Year hawker bazaar to take place on a Mong Kok playground, as long as hawkers cooked only with electricity, rather than gas-fuelled woks or charcoal. The local district co[illegible]deemed the proposal unworkable and voted it down. 'It tells you a lot about the mentality of those in power,' said Mo. 'They think that to play it safe you should do nothing.' Despite its promise to be open-minded, the government is filled with people who think that the old policy of elimination through attrition was correct. Most people who own hawker licenses are old now. They are the last generation, and the government knows it.

What's needed is more than a policy fix – it's a wholesale change of culture. Hong Kong has changed, but the people who run it haven't. They're working from an outdated textbook. The Umbrella Movement generation isn't necessarily upset because apartments are unaffordable and they can't find high-paying jobs. They're upset because a new set of values has emerged, one that places happiness on a higher pedestal than material wealth and doesn't jibe with the government's policies. Though Hong Kong's establishment remains as conservative as ever, Hong Kong's youth are in the midst of a cultural transformation as many grow disenchanted with the city's authoritarian politics and oligarchic economy. Many young people are leading deliberately eccentric lives, opening bookstores in public markets, settling in rural squatter villages and running hawker stalls where they sell locally farmed fruit. In a city where government control feels oppressive, where the political system denies them representation, these activities are a way to reclaim their identity as citizens.

*

On an impossibly muggy day in August, I made my way up to the northern New Territories, near the border with mainland China, where the skyscrapers of Shenzhen soar incongruously over mudflats and mangrove swamps. I was there to meet with Tam Chi-kit, known to his friends as Kit Jai, who grows bananas and sells them at Kai Fong Pai Dong. Tam grew up in a rural village, and he has been involved in land activism for awhile, trying to protect the rights of small-scale squatter farmers whose land is owned by the government and huge property conglomerates. During the final weeks of Occupy, he met Uncle Wong, a 90-year-old democracy activist, and Uncle Chan, a garrulous 70-something man with a toothy grin. The three of them decided to revive Wong's farm, which had been left fallow.

The farm wasn't what I expected. It's a muddy acre of land that spills down a hill to the Sheung Yue River. There are banana trees, but also papayas, soursop and an abundance of herbs. Walking down a concrete path past two metal gates, we arrived at a cluster of tin-roofed structures where I met Uncle Chan, Uncle Wong and Auntie Wong. Tam filled me in on the details. Uncle Wong was born in China and raised in Indonesia, but as a young man he returned to his homeland and worked for the government. Eventually, he became disillusioned with the Communist regime and fled to Hong Kong. 'By then, all of the good land was taken, so the only thing he could find was this place on a hillside,' says Tam.

Wong built a pitched-roof house, which he expanded bit by bit, eventually constructing a huge shed that covered the entire structure. I marvelled at the construction as we sat around a large table. Auntie Wong served us soup made with papaya grown on the farm, while Chan brought out a steamed fish he had caught that morning in the river. He poured us glasses of wine. Tam leaned over and explained that it was Chan who had started the carpentry workshop that built all the street furniture at Occupy, including the brilliant steps over the highway barriers. I asked him why he was inspired to start building the furniture. He shrugged modestly. 'I used to work in construction, so when I saw kids needed tables to study, it just went from there.'

These are the kinds of unexpected connections that happen when people are given a chance to build their own city. People become active participants in civic life, not passive occupants of someone else's space. When they're given the chance, few people are as good at making fascinating spaces as Hong Kongers. The creative energy that infused the streets during the Umbrella Movement didn't disappear after the occupation ended; it dispersed. You can see it in the improvised shelters of Duckling Hill, in the neighbourhood bonds built in every street market. And you can see in the Western District Public Cargo Working Area, which, despite its unwieldy name, is one of the city's most interesting self-organised spaces.

Kids call it the Instagram Pier, because it's a photogenic expanse of concrete soaked in briny puddles, surrounded by rusty boats and the cerulean waters of

Victoria Harbour. A wide range of people from across the west side of Hong Kong Island come here for refuge from the crowded streets and stagnant city air. One evening, I wandered onto the pier, past a sternly worded 'keep out' sign wholly ignored by the stream of people making their way towards the water.

The pier is particularly lively during Mid-Autumn Festival, when families gather to barbecue next to the water; some even bring portable generators and small televisions to sing karaoke. But it's a popular place on any night. As I made my way down the pier, a group of runners bounded past, swerving to avoid a poodle tugging at its leash. The smell of marijuana drifted on the sea breeze. A cluster of Korean students sat on the pavement, drinking beer as their legs dangled over the edge. An elderly woman walked past, methodically slapping her arms to improve her circulation. A teenager filmed his friends as they attempted skateboard tricks. After a few minutes, I reached the edge of the pier, where two friends were strumming guitars. A group of middle-aged women sat on plastic crates, chatting in Hokkien, eyeing a young girl looping around the pier on her bicycle. A couple had laid out a blanket and they were sitting cross-legged, holding hands, an open bottle of champagne and some cake next to them. Waves sloshed against concrete as ferries and fishing boats motored past.

You could spend hours cataloguing all the different activities on the pier. You could amuse yourself by noting everything you see that would be banned in a normal Hong Kong park: smoking, skateboarding, cycling, barbecuing, dog-walking, even – believe it or not – guitar-strumming. Here, people were free, and you could feel it in the air.

Why Does This Matter?

In 1961, Jane Jacobs published *The Death and Life of Great American Cities*, a seminal text that re-evaluated the city through the eyes of a keenly observant citizen – a woman on the street, not a man in an office. Writing about her neighbourhood on Hudson Street in Greenwich Village, she pointed out the importance of having a diversity of buildings (old and new, smart and shabby) dedicated to a mixed range of uses (retail, offices, apartments, workshops) in sustaining the life of a dynamic city like New York. Here in Hong Kong, the area around Kai Fong Pai Dong feels a lot like Jacobs' Hudson Street: a panoply of market stalls and small businesses, butchers who greet regular customers as they pass by, hawkers trading in the dried herbs and fruits necessary for healthy Chinese soup.

These things come naturally to urban spaces when they are allowed to respond to the people who use them. 'If you want to seed a place with activity, the first thing to do is to put out food,' wrote William H. Whyte in his book, *City: Rediscovering the Center.*[24] After examining hours of film footage of New York public spaces, Whyte noted that lively public spaces create a virtuous cycle of deliciousness, drawing hawkers to the crowds, which in turn draws more people to the space. Whyte also pointed out how governments often seem wilfully blind to the way hawkers are harbingers of good urban spaces. Hawkers are often banned from the places where they do the most business, and if they are allowed, they are subject to stringent regulations.

Whyte's statements, like Jacobs', apply to the Hong Kong of today, but Whyte wrote that book in 1988. Since then, many of the world's cities have come to recognise the benefits of informal urban life, and have reformed their policies accordingly. Food trucks have been allowed to flourish in Los Angeles, where they transform dreary strip malls into late-night eateries. New York has turned a number of its most prominent streets and intersections into pedestrian plazas, filled with loose tables and chairs. Melbourne has spent decades turning derelict alleyways into some of the city's liveliest public spaces. In Montreal, citizens converted a vacant lot into a lush garden, and the government – after initially trying to clear the site – made it an official public space, albeit one managed by the citizens themselves.

GUIDE TO THE MUSÉE D'ART MODERNE DE LA VILLE DE PARIS

PARIS musées
LES MUSÉES DE LA VILLE DE PARIS

LES AMIS
du musée
d'art moderne
de la ville de Paris

This work is a revised, corrected and supplemented re-edition
of the général Guide to the musée d'Art moderne de la Ville de Paris
(1998), complete with new texts.

DIRECTOR OF PUBLICATION:
Suzanne Pagé
COORDINATION:
Juliette Laffon, Gérard Audinet
with Camille Morineau
HISTORY OF THE MUSEUM:
Suzanne Pagé
with Jean-Louis Andral and François Michaud
INTRODUCTION TO THE CONTEMPORARY COLLECTION:
Béatrice Parent (B.P.)
TEXTS WRITTEN BY:
Gérard Audinet (G.A.)
Martine Contensou (M.C.)
Cécile Debray (C.D.)
Emmanuelle de l'Ecotais (E.E.)
Gladys Fabre (G.F.)
Dominique Gagneux (D.G.)
Sophie Krebs (S.K.)
Juliette Laffon (J.L.)
Camille Morineau (C.M.)
Jacqueline Munck (J.M.)
Miriam Simon (M.S.)

CONTENTS

P.10 PREFACE

INTRODUCTION

P.14 HISTORY OF A MUSEUM THROUGH ITS BUILDING
P.30 MAJOR BEQUESTS

MODERN ART COLLECTION

1900-1960

P.36 FAUVISM · P.44 GEORGES ROUAULT
P.48 CUBISM AND ITS LEGACY · P.64 FERNAND LÉGER
P.68 ROBERT DELAUNAY · P.74 DADA AND SURREALISM
P.88 JEAN CROTTI · P.90 VICTOR BRAUNER
P.94 ABSTRACTION BETWEEN THE WARS
P.102 THE SCHOOL OF PARIS · P.112 MARCEL GROMAIRE

P.114 RAOUL DUFY · P.118 PIERRE BONNARD
P.122 ÉDOUARD VUILLARD · P.124 JEAN FAUTRIER
P.130 FIGURATIONS, NON-FIGURATIONS
P.136 ABSTRACTIONS

MONUMENTAL WORKS

P.148 LA DANSE, HENRI MATISSE · P.158 LA FÉE ÉLECTRICITÉ, RAOUL DUFY · P.164 RÉALITÉS NOUVELLES

CONTEMPORARY ART COLLECTION

P.179 ORIENTATIONS
P.206 INDEX

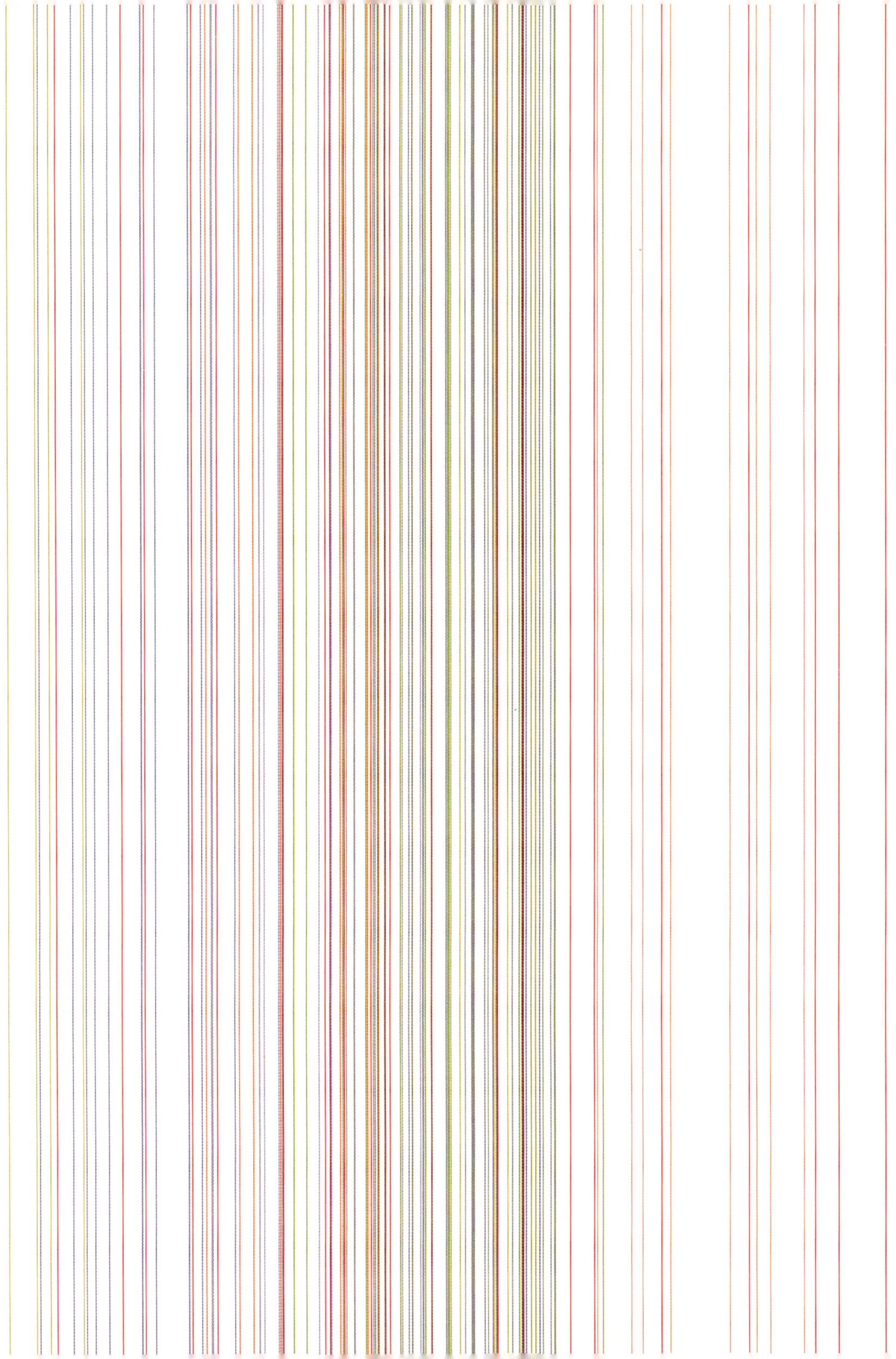

PREFACE

SUZANNE PAGÉ

First and foremost, the Musée d'Art Moderne de la Ville de Paris owes its reputation to its exhibitions. Both the "historical" overviews devoted to modern European art[1] and its major figures[2], and targeted contemporary events organized by the ARC[3] – whose creation in 1967 was a decisive turning point for the institution – have had a national and international impact. These exhibitions created a venue that welcomed new, unusual and even provocative concepts; they altered peoples' awareness and ways of seeing, leading to critical reinterpretations of history, and challenging accepted ideas and boundaries. This program of exhibitions is legitimized through a constant state of confrontation with the specific context of collection.

Hence, the presence of reference works, of a "memory" in the museum, is responsible for the unique mobilization of artists themselves – this, of course, is necessarily a part of history, if only as a way for artists to position themselves in relation to it. This collection in the Musée d'Art Moderne has its own characteristics and gaps, as well as its strong points – all of which contribute to its originality.

Strongly anchored to the history of Paris, this collection started with the creation of the museum itself, designed as part of the 1937 Universal Exhibition of Arts and Techniques, although it only opened in 1961 with, notably, a core of works from the "modern" collections of the Petit Palais. The generosity of such collectors as Emanuele Sarmiento, Mathilde Amos, and Ambroise Vollard was also a major factor for the museum. Picasso's donation of his *Evocation* (1901) created the chronological limits of the collection. The 1937 exhibition was notable in terms of particularly remarkable acquisitions. Works that entered the museum collection include Matisse's *La Danse*, Bonnard's *Nu dans le bain* and *Le Jardin*, Robert Delaunay's *L'Equipe de Cardiff*, Derain's *La Rivière*, Léger's *Les Disques*, Lhote's *Escale*, Metzinger's *L'Oiseau bleu*, four *Portraits* of artists by Vuillard, as well as furniture from Pierre Chareau, André Arbus and Adnet, which are still counted among the museum's masterpieces. Other large decorative works by Robert and Sonia Delaunay, Albert Gleizes and Jacques Villon were acquired as part of the same movement (gift from the Salon des réalités nouvelles in 1939). The addition of the Giradin bequest in 1953 was decisive in the decision on the part of the Parisian authorities to expand beyond the cramped wall of the Petit Palais to open a separate space within the Palais de Tokyo.

Our museum then embarked on a slow conquest of its own territory, while working within the limits of scheduling that were foreign to its own mission: the "musée du Costume," for example, was temporary housed in the museum until 1971, while numerous and diverse Salons – not all of which were highly "professional" – also used the premises.

Since the collection finally reclaimed its space – which has been definitive in 1989 – the works have been exhibited on the lower ground floor of the museum, serving as a symbolic foundation to a building structured around two major decorative works. One is the monumental painting by Dufy, *La Fée Electricité*, created for the Palais du Pavillon de l'Electricité et de la Lumière, designed by Mallet-Stevens for the 1937 International Exhibition, and transferred to the museum in 1964 (a gift from Electricité de France). The other essential work is Henri Matisse's *La Danse* (the so-called "Paris" version, 1931-33), reinstalled in 1990 according to the artist's original specifications. The fortunate discovery in

1993 of the first version of this work, entitled *La Danse inachevée, 1931* was a notable addition. The comparison between a "hand-painted" version and another one based on cut-out papers and a more minimalist esthetic, is particularly significant for art history – especially as Daniel Buren pursued this vein in a recent presentation, *Murs de Peinture* (1995). These series of contemporary "installation" is a specific focus within the collection, which receives new impetus from these incursions by artists who confront the museum with itself and its history. Examples of this include Christian Boltanski's work on the basement level (*Réserve du Musée des enfants*) and Niele Toroni's *Cabinet de peinture*. This strategy strengthens the difference sought by putting forward the museum's strong points and recognized ensembles.

Over the last fifteen years, a specific acquisitions policy has been established with the aim of defining the museum's identity. Because Paris already has a national institution entrusted with an international and even a "global" mission, we have limited our scope to a Paris-based European priority, and the formation of significant ensembles based on a movement or a figure. This decision arose from the origins and history of our collections, which owes much to private donations of works acquired in Paris. The Henry-Thomas donation is a good example, as is Madeleine Lacourière's donation of Picasso's *Suite Vollard*, and in 2003, Aube Elléouët's donation as part of the André Breton sale). We have also received gifts from artists, all of which reinforced the museum's strong engagements. This artwork includes the Georges Rouault and Marcel Gromaire ensemble (Girardin bequest), Jean Crotti's ensemble (Suzanne Duchamp bequest), Victor Brauner ensemble (Jacqueline Brauner bequest), works by Jean Fautrier, Bryon Gysin and even more recently, Simon Hantaï, Pierre Soulages, Niele Toroni, Aurélie Nemours, Erró, Christian Boltanski, Fabrice Hybert, Bertrand Lavier, Peter Fischli and David Weiss. These were all generous gestures on the part of the artists, who have had a decisive impact on the institution.

The museum's explicit desire is now to develop a historical dimension, and, with a few exceptions, to expand the important core collections (Fautrier) in a lucid way, rather than filling in the gaps; and to develop the collections from the 1960s on, by promoting a policy of temporary exhibitions that reveal offer a more intimate understanding of artists and their works. Hence, thanks to a systematic effort, major movements such as Nouveau Réalisme, Nouvelle Figuration, Supports-Surfaces in France and Arte Povera in Italy are now fully represented. And this has been extended to include extremely contemporary figures who work with all the various supports available to "plastic" artists today: from Louise Bourgeois to Annette Messager, from Bertrand Lavier to Bernard Frize, from Fabrice Hybert to Claude Lévêque, from Pierre Huyghe to Philippe Parreno, Dominique Gonzalez-Foerster, Mélik Ohanian, Anri Sala and so on; and on a European level, from Hanne Darboven to Sigmar Polke and Gerhart Richter, Gilbert and George, John Armleder, Hans Peter Feldman; from Jan Dibbets to Thomas Schutte, Ettore Spaletti, Jan Vercruysse, Olafur Eliasson, David Claerbout, Rosemarie Trockel, Tacita Dean...

The City of Paris[4] has its renewed commitment to its heritage through recent acquisitions; this reinforces the participation of private donors, particularly artists themselves, whose generosity has been constant. As a result, new works have significantly enriched the museum, fully justifying the publication of this new guide ▪

1. Expressionnism in Germany, Beauté exacte (Holland), Lumière du Nord (ScanPays Scandinaves), Fauvisme.
2. Such as Alberto Giacometti, André Derain, El Lissitzky, Mark Rothko, Alexander Calder, Francis Picabia.
3. From Mario Merz to Jannis Kounellis, Sol Lewitt to Agnès Martin, Christian Boltanski and Daniel Buren to Pierre Huyghe, Parreno and Dominique Gonzalez-Foerster, along with Sigmar Polke, Georg Bazelitz, Nam June Paik to Olafur Eliasson, Gilbert and George, Louise Bourgeois to Annette Messager, Gerhart Richter, Robert Filliou, Claude Lévêque, Jean-Marc Bustamante, Anri Sala and more provocative approachese, *L'Hiver de l'Amour*, Matthew Barney, etc.
4. In the captions for artwork, we have indicated "purchase" for the acquisitions, which are all purchases on the part of the City of Paris.

INTRO DUCTION

PIERRE JAHAN MUSÉE D'ART MODERNE DE PARIS, 1937.
17.7 X 18.5 CM. DONATED IN 1985.

HISTORY OF A MUSEUM
THROUGH ITS BUILDING

Between the two world wars, the contemporary artistic scene in Paris had to make do with a legacy of institutional museums left over from the nineteenth century. One such was the Musée du Luxembourg, the first museum of modern art, created in 1818 by Louis XVIII to display works by living artists. Since 1886 it had been housed in the Orangerie du Luxembourg.

The premises soon proved far too small for the collections, and the works had to be transferred. The first to go were those by foreign artists; in 1922 they were moved moved to the Jeu de Paume, renamed ten years later the Musée des Écoles Étrangères Contemporaines. Then in 1927-28, the Caillebotte bequest and recognized French works were given to the Louvre.

The City of Paris exhibited its collection in its own museum, the Palais des Beaux-Arts de la Ville de Paris, which was inaugurated in 1901 within the Petit Palais, erected for the Universal Exhibition in 1900.

Contemporary art was therefore divided and housed within old-fashioned, insufficient or unsuitable buildings, at a time when the new science of museology was stressing the need for more appropriate spaces.

Back in 1899, the curator of the Luxembourg, Léonce Benedite, had requested a new museum, an idea supported by the Société des Amis du Luxembourg, created in 1903. Twenty years went by before the "Exposition internationale des arts décoratifs et industriels modernes" (International Exhibition of Modern Decorative and Industrial Arts), set up in 1925, raised the question of just what the museums had to offer the public. The debate was relaunched in the form of a survey conducted by the magazine *L'Art vivant*[1]. In 1925, it published the replies of sixty-four figures from the art world – artists, critics, collectors, dealers, writers and journalists – to two questions: "What do you think of the idea of a French museum of modern art?" and "Which ten living artists – painters or sculptors – should feature initially?" The emphasis on the idea of a French school was symptomatic of the time; indeed, despite repeated pleas by curator André Dezarrois, the collection of the Musée des Écoles Etrangères – which should logically have complemented the work of the École Française – remained at the Jeu de Paume until the late 1930s. It was not until 1947 that these works joined the Musée National d'Art Moderne and were housed in the west wing of the palais de Tokyo.

The survey clearly illustrated the failure of the Luxembourg's original mission – to become the "Museum of Living Artists" – as the acquisitions still favored the academic style of the Salons. It also ushered in the idea of a modern museum, an idea promoted in 1928 by Louis Hautecœur, both within the international museum department and at the Musée du Luxembourg (where he became curator shortly after). He devised a number of solutions, which all encountered administrative hurdles, before coming up with his first plans for a new museum in 1932.

Meanwhile the Petit Palais museum was running out of space. To its curator, Raymond Escholier, the focus of the museum had become unclear, as the early collections of the 1902 Dutuit bequest were at odds with the contemporary works, and he wanted a new building for living artists ■

THE PROGRAM: ONE BUILDING FOR TWO MUSEUMS

In the early 1930s, there seemed therefore to be a general consensus in favor of the creation in Paris of a truly representative museum of modern art.

The pretext came in the shape of the forthcoming “Exposition Internationale des Arts et Techniques dans la Vie Moderne” (International Exhibition of Arts and Techniques in Modern Life). Events of this kind always leave behind a legacy of facilities, essentially cultural ones, and it seemed feasible to incorporate the missing museum, which had become essential.

On January 16, 1933, a decree stated that the Exhibition would take place in 1937. It also defined the sections: the decorative and industrial arts, intellectual cooperation, work and agricultural life. Two months later, the Paris Council proposed setting up the exhibition in the center of Paris, on the banks of the Seine, between the Alexandre-III and Iéna bridges.

All that was needed was a framework for collaboration between the city and the state, and a choice of sites and assignments. In May of 1934, both parties signed an agreement; article 6 stipulated the conditions for the creation of not one but two museums of modern art. At long last, Raymond Escholier’s goal and Louis Hautecœur’s aim were realized. The government donated the land of the former Manufacture of Savonnerie carpets, which the military had been using since 1836 as the Manutention building. It was situated between Avenue du Président-Wilson and the Quai de Tokyo. Two museums of identical size were planned. One was to be given to the city of Paris, which agreed to provide the major share of financing. The original state museum therefore found itself with an additional twin municipal museum, the result of a financial agreement that would, in time, become more balanced.

In August 1934, Louis Hautecœur reviewed his building plans for "the construction of museums of modern art to house the collections of the State and the City of Paris." He began by saying that "The Museum of the City of Paris is designed to contain works of modern art in the fields of sculpture, painting, architecture and the applied arts. It will serve as an annex to the Petit Palais and will represent the equivalent surface area and volume as the State Museum." An architectural competition was launched mid-September: "The general curatorial committee of the 1937 Exhibition is launching a competition among French architects to devise a project for the construction of two Museums of Modern Art on the sites currently occupied by the military Manutention in the Avenue de Tokio [sic] and in the Avenue du Président-Wilson"

THE PROJECT

The anonymous projects were submitted to a jury of fifty-seven people from November 30, and the results were announced on December 24, 1934[2].

The 128 proposals represented over 300 architects, including the greatest names of the time: Mallet-Stevens; Le Corbusier; Tony-Garnier; and the Boileau, Azéma and Carlu trio, shortly to design the new Trocadéro. The "Clarity" project was finally selected. A plan of classical sobriety, in keeping with current taste, it was designed by two young architects, Jean-Claude Dondel and André Aubert, in association with two older architects, Paul Viard and Marcel Dastugue. The uneven terrain and the slopes led the designers to create a wide breach between the two museums, creating a view of the Seine. Two landings were connected by a colonnade that formed a portico around a large patio, with wide staircases leading to the terraces around the ornamental basin. The terraces led out along the bank of the Seine, its level attained at the axis of the breach by vast stairways. Finally, the outside areas

CONSTRUCTION SITE FOR THE MODERN ART MUSEUMS.

were designed to exhibit sculptures.Inside, the differences in level allowed the architects to create highly diverse volumes. The lighting aspect of the program had envisaged overhead light for the painting galleries; the architects said they were inspired by recent Dutch museums – the Gemeente Museum in the Hague and the Boymans-van Beuningen in Rotterdam – and new installations in London's National Gallery. The overhead lighting provided uniform illumination to all the exhibition areas via glass ceilings. This uniformity was particularly difficult to obtain in the ground floor rooms, as the ceiling did not open directly on the outside. Along the Rue de la Manutention and the Rue Gaston-de-Saint-Paul, the gallery was arranged in comb-like rooms, due to the length required for the painting rails; this design brought more daylight into the rooms. It was reflected by grooves in the frosted glass ceiling, avoiding the drawback of partitions that often create backlighting or overly harsh illumination. The sculpture galleries, on the other hand, were bathed in lateral daylight from their high windows. Apart from the basement rooms, linked by a wide transverse service road with access for trucks, only one common facility was planned: a conference room with projection facilities seating 250 people, situated beneath the portico and only used once, the day of the inauguration.

Louis Hautecœur remarked that “the only difference between these twin museums is that the difference in levels gives a more squat appearance to the one belonging to the City of Paris.” Plans here included the construction of a “grand reception hall” within the museum itself[3].

Reactions were far from unanimous, and in the January 1935 edition of *L'Architecture d'aujourd'hui*, Le Corbusier, whose ambitious project had not even obtained a distinction, wrote: “The prize has not been awarded to museums, but to a street, a dreary little street one hundred meters long, a trench just like the thousands of other trenches which furrow through Paris.”

Criticism was mostly leveled at the program itself, with particular emphasis on the question “Why two museums?” Raymond Escholier even wondered: “Are these two museums of modern art not going to overlap? It is quite obvious that only one museum should have been erected on the Quai de Tokio [sic], the one belonging to the city of Paris, which owns the land. Would it not have been wiser to leave the state museum on the left bank, in the vicinity of the Luxembourg, within the former Saint-Sulpice seminary?
Such hypotheses, however, belong to the past, and one must, indeed should, admit that art and artists can only benefit from the proximity of these two museums and the emulation between city and state...” Opinions remained divided as to whether this was an unfortunate overlap or a healthy partnership between two institutions. But an element of variety was introduced in an agreement stating that the plastic arts should have priority in the state museum whereas the municipal museum would give precedence to the decorative arts, “the arts of Parisian life” — a convenient division which was naturally never respected

THE BUILDING SITE

On January 1, 1935 the winning architects finalized their project, only to adjust it in March, when it was decided to add on the land belonging to the Polish Embassy mansion. This created an enclave in the construction site at the corner of the Quai de Tokyo and the Rue Gaston-de-Saint-Paul, particularly on the city museum side. The demolition of the Manutention began on March 10, 1935 and was completed on April 30. On July 5, President Albert Lebrun of France ceremonially laid the first stone.

The building schedule estimated contributions from twenty different trades and over one thousand workers per day, involving the preparation of materials in the factories and quarries and their installation on the site. The foundations were completed on April 30, 1936, with over two thousand concrete piles set in a sandbank situated sixteen meters underground to support the reinforced concrete framework. The Polish Embassy was demolished at the same time, and the first concrete foundations were poured on March 15.

As the facades were erected in long simple lines and covered in comblanchien, massangis and travertine limestone, the commissioned artists began making their contributions to this classical structure. A large bas-relief by Alfred Janniot — who had already decorated the Palais des Colonies in 1931 — flanked the outside staircase in the form of an allegory praising the Arts; on the two Seine-facing wings, Léon Baudry and Marcel Gaumont offset the austerity of the tall windows with metopes featuring centaurs and water nymphs. The two bronze monumental doors of the museums on the Avenue du Président-Wilson were entrusted to André Bizette-Lindet and Gabriel Forestier, while Louis-Jules Dideron conceived an allegory of the City of Paris for the door of the municipal museum on the Quai de Tokyo. The *Apollo* originally designed by Charles Despiau to adorn the center of the upper piazza, which he was unable

CA 1937, CONSTRUCTION OF THE MUSEUM, VIEWED FROM THE LOWER TERRACE.

to finish in time, was replaced by Antoine Bourdelle's imposing bronze, the *Génie de la France.* On the lower piazza, Félix-Pascal Févola's fountain supplied water for the ornamental basin surrounded with recumbent figures by Léon Drivier, Auguste Guénot and Louis Dejean, and featured statues from André Abbal, Georges Chauvel, René Collamarini, Jean-René Debarre, Louis-Aimé Lejeune, Charles Malfray, Jean Osouf, Émile-François Popineau, Anna Quinquaud, Georges Saupique, Paul Simon and Pierre Vigoureux ■

THE INAUGURATION OF THE 1937 EXHIBITION

The modern art museums were inaugurated by President Lebrun on May 24, 1937. In the state wing, the director of the Beaux-Arts, Georges Huisman, had set up an exhibition devoted to "Chefs d'œuvres de l'art français" (Masterpieces of French Art).

Meanwhile, the city museum was offering a range of exhibitions. On the lower-ground floor, the Paris Pavilion retraced the history of the capital and surrounding area through maps and paintings. On the upper ground floor, a number of events depicted the approaches of three museums to museography. The "art" museum had an exhibition devoted to "The Life and Work of Van Gogh," devised by René Huyghe, with Michel Florisoone and John Rewald. The "historical" museum held an exhibition on theater in the Middle Ages, by Gustave Cohen. The "scientific" museum, with Georges-Henri Rivière, depicted the rural French home. Finally, a section showed ways that museums make themselves known through "popularization" and "propaganda." Upstairs, an exhibition on "Intellectual exchanges throughout the world" had been set up by Louis Gallié and Georges-Henri Rivière and designed by Jean Lurçat and André Vigneau.
As intended, the general commissariat of the exhibition was housed in the grand reception hall, in a setting conceived by Halley.

1937, THE PALAIS DE TOKYO, VIEWED FROM THE QUAI DE TOKYO.

1938-1954

The 1937 exhibition that closed on November 25 was a great success despite severe financial losses. Forty-four nations had taken part and over 31 million visitors had attended. Its legacy, two museums of modern art, could now concentrate on their true vocation.

The municipal museum was handed over on August 1, 1938. The city put in a claim for non-completion of the building, but despite repeated demands, the government never granted the funding required to carry out the completion work needed to use the building as planned. The premises therefore remained vacant until 1940.

Starting in 1941, the municipal wing of the Palais de Tokyo was made available to an association, L'Entraide des artistes, so that it could hold artistic salons that could no longer use the Grand Palais, and thus avoid the threat of requisition. A series of Salons were held there, including the Salon des Indépendants, the Salon des Artistes Français, the Salon des Tuileries, the Salon du Dessin, designed to occupy the premises over the summer, the Salon d'Automne and the Salon d'Hiver.

In August of 1943, several months after occupying the basements of the Musée National d'Art Moderne, the German authorities requisitioned the basements of the municipal museum, where they stored crates of clothing, personal effects and plundered property[4].

At the Liberation, the basements were placed at the disposal of various organizations and were put to a number of uses: a warehouse for provincial stained-glass windows, a depot for stuffed animals from the Levallois-Perret Museum, a storeroom for maps and documents from the Ministry for Reconstruction and Urbanism, a customs warehouse and a storeroom for sets from the Renaud-Barrault theater company. A number of the Salons returned to the Grand Palais while others remained in the Musée d'Art Moderne de la Ville de Paris

1937, ENTRANCE TO THE CITY OF PARIS PAVILION FOR THE INTERNATIONAL EXHIBITION.

1954-1961

Dr. Maurice Girardin's 1953 bequest, which was shown to the public at the Petit Palais in 1954, revealed how inadequate this building was for displaying modern art, particularly in view of the fact that another museum was designed to do just that. First and foremost, however, space had to be cleared by emptying the basements in order to install a storeroom. The Salons were limited to the upper-ground floor and first floor so that the modern art collection could be displayed on the lower-ground floor. Substantial improvements were made in 1954 on the latter level: staircases were removed, new means of access were provided, the galleries were rearranged and the ceilings were lowered.

Finally, in the so-called "dark-room" (now known as the "Salle Matisse"), the collections and exhibitions of the Musée du Costume were displayed from 1956 through 1971.

After six years of construction, the Musée d'Art Moderne de la Ville de Paris was inaugurated on July 6, 1961 with the modern art collection from the Petit Palais and the collection donated by Dr. Girardin. In 1964, Raoul Dufy's *Fée Électricité*, designed for the Electricity and Lighting Pavilion at the 1937 Exhibition, was hung in the "Great Hall."

The building, which housed the first Biennale de Paris in 1959, continued to host a great many Salons — Salon de Mai, Salon des Réalités Nouvelles, Salon de la Jeune Peinture — as well as the Salon des Médecins, Club International Féminin and Association de la Préfecture de Police. In order to show off the museum's collection to full advantage several solutions were devised, including, in 1966, the installation in the basements of an exhibition room specially designed for such events, with independent access for visits, on the Quai de New York. ■

CONSTRUCTION WORK 1971-1972 AND 1992-1994

Meanwhile — as the ARC was being created within the museum — the Paris Council decided in 1967 to launch a new building program. Work began in January 1971 under Pierre Faucheux and Michel Jausserand and was completed in May 1972. The rooms on the upper-ground floor were altered by freeing the framework of the building from the numerous internal partitions; by eliminating the stairways as much as possible and replacing them with ramps; and by creating new levels and providing technical equipment to provide a certain degree of flexibility. The initial plan was modified by the creation of a floor dividing the former entrance hall, a mezzanine for the offices and documentation center, an auditorium connected to the new galleries by a split-level passageway and an elevator linking each floor of the museum. The Wilson gallery had a specific surface area, limited by a fixed ceiling, whereas the New York gallery contained mobile ceilings to create more flexible spaces, although this turned out to be unworkable in practice. Triangular frames of tubular casing on the floor were destined to hold pillars for adjustable partitions. This "mobile" museographical concept was typical of the period with its striking use of space, but was soon to reveal its drawbacks. The ARC, which had moved around to various rooms in the museum, found a permanent home in the upper floor rooms.

Twenty years later, funds were once more made available to revise the air conditioning system in the temporary exhibition rooms on the upper-ground floor and to provide wheelchair access. This gave the new museum director the opportunity to continue the rehabilitation program, first set up in 1989, when the exhibition "Histoires de musée" revealed the building's hidden qualities to a wide public. The operation, which took place between 1991 and 1994 under the aegis of architect Jean-François Bodin, returned a number of areas to their original sizes — such as the threshold of the Président-Wilson entrance — by reducing as far as possible the gradients on the upper-ground floor and by exploiting the maximum dimensions of the exhibition halls, getting rid of a number of obsolete elements and introducing a new lighting system. The acquisition of Matisse's rediscovered version of *La Danse Inachevée* in 1993, which was to hang opposite his *Danse de Paris,* in the collections since 1937, made a specific room necessary, with the requisite measurements. This explains why the dark-room, now known as the "Salle Matisse," was also modified during the construction work, and now permanently features the two triptychs by one of the leading artists of the twentieth century. Since then, temporary exhibitions have provided an opportunity to systematically reconstitute the volumes according to their original concept, so that the lowerground floor could be gradually renovated. With the exhibition entitled "Les Années 30 en Europe : le temps menaçant, 1929-1939" (Threatening Times — The Thirties in Europe — 1929-1939), the main staircase, which initially led to all the levels, was uncovered and made accessible to the public once again.

This is how this museum of modern and contemporary art appears today, sixty-five years after its inauguration. The gradual and complete restoration of its original architecture has been undertaken in an attempt to grant it a privileged role, both in the context of Paris and Europe and in the world of contemporary creation, and to provide it with a recognized and specific identity ■

Suzanne Pagé and **Jean-Louis Andral**

Suzanne Pagé would like to thank **François Michaud** for his work updating the research in the archives.

1. *Pour un musée français d'art moderne, une enquête de l'Art vivant en 1925,* documents gathered by Jean-Paul Morel, Paris, R.M.N., Séguier, 1996.
2. Bertrand Lemoine, "Le Palais de Tokyo," in *Les années 30 en Europe : le temps menaçant 1929-1929,* Musée d'Art Moderne de la Ville de Paris, February 25-May 25, 1997. BrunoFoucart, Jean-Baptiste Minnaert, "Les Musées d'Art Moderne," in Paris, 1937, *Paris 1937, cinquantenaire de l'Exposition internationale des arts et des techniques dans la via moderne,* IFA, Musée d'Art Moderne de la Ville de Paris, May 13-August 30, 1987.
3. This room was one of the key elements of the design conceived by the City of Paris, which wanted to create a majestic room for illustrious guests. A report from the City Council, signed by the Prefect of the Seine on December 17, 1936, stipulated the dual role that the City of Paris would have to play during the exhibition: first, "to officially host the many eminent figures who come to visit the Exhibition"; and second, as exhibitor, "to demonstrate the work achieved in terms of urbanization and the development of the capital toward a larger Paris."
4. Yvon Bizardel, *Sous l'Occupation, souvenirs d'un conservateur de musée,* Paris, Calmann-Lévy, 1964, pp. 147-149. Archives of the Musée d'Art Moderne de la Ville de Paris.

MAJOR BEQUESTS

The Petit Palais, Musée des Beaux-Arts de la Ville de Paris, received its first significant donations in the 1930s, and these played a vital role in the future collections of the Musée d'Art Moderne. The first came from Emanuele Sarmiento. Born in Rome to Colombian parents of Italian origin, he was the Colombian Consul in Italy before settling in Paris in 1914. Between the wars he became involved with Italian artists in Paris – including the productive Mario Tozzi – in the role of coordinator and benefactor. Equally receptive to the "figuration" of an artist such as De Pisis as to the futurist "aeropainting" of Prampolini, he helped organize a number of events. Following the major exhibition of Italian art in 1935 in the Jeu de Paume and Petit Palais Museums, in 1936 he gave the latter fifty-five works by Italian artists and by the group known as the School of Paris. This collection was transferred to the Musée d'Art Moderne when it opened.

In 1937, Ambroise Vollard donated a remarkable collection of ceramics, decorated by the painters of the School of Asnières, and some illustrated books, which joined the two bronzes by Picasso (*Fernande* and *Le Fou*) already donated. Later, the museum received the famous painting from Picasso's Blue period, EVOCATION, (ca 1901).

EVOCATİON, CA 1901. OIL ON CANVAS, 150.5 X 90.5 CM.
DONATED BY THE ESTATE OF AMBROISE VOLLARD, 1950.

PABLO PİCASSO

After the war, the extent of the bequest by Dr. Maurice Girardin (1884-1951) precipitated the transfer of twentieth-century works from the Petit Palais and the inauguration of the Musée d'Art Moderne in the Palais de Tokyo in 1961. A dental surgeon, collector and benefactor, he opened the Licorne gallery in 1921 and took up publishing. In 1920 he signed a contract with Gromaire, granting him exclusive rights over the latter's production. He also supported Maria Blanchard, became an ardent Georges Rouault enthusiast and bought up almost all Bernard Buffet's early works. Dr. Girardin also loved African and Oceanian art and bequeathed a significant collection of these works. Back in the 1920s, he offered a donation to the Petit Palais, but reservations on the part of certain artists prevented it from going through. His collection of five hundred works, bequeathed to the City of Paris, was accepted in 1953, after his death.

The 1955 Amos donation, which entered the museum in 1967 (Dufy), and the considerable Henry-Thomas collection made a decisive contribution to the museum's identity. The collectors Germaine Henry (1904-1997) and Professor Robert Thomas (1900-1989), both discreet to the point of secrecy, offered the majority of the works they owned in a series of donations (1976, 1984, 1986), under the general title of the Henry-Thomas collection. This completed the Fauve and Cubist collections and also provided the museum with its first works by Picabia and Kupka. There were many canvases by Delaunay and Herbin, but the collection also spanned the post-war figurative and abstract art movements. An entire room is reserved for this donation, although some works have been placed elsewhere to emphasize chronological continuity in the presentation of the permanent collections.

Today, following the example of many private collectors, a number of artists and their families have been exceptional generous and continue to make an active contribution to the museum's collections ■

G.A.

MODERN ART COLLECTION

FAUVISM

The decisive move towards the emancipation of color as the consecration of Fauvism, the first aesthetic revolution of the twentieth century, involved communicating the energy and expressive quality of pure color on to canvas, as well as celebrating its luminosity and constructing a simplified space.

Fauvism, an ironic term coined by the critic Louis Vauxcelles, "officially" saw the light of day at the 1905 Salon d'Automne, and was supported by Ambroise Vollard, Berthe Weill and Eugène Druet. It represented a group of artists rather than an actual movement. It drew together the former pupils of Gustave Moreau, Matisse, Manguin, Camoin (...) and those of Eugène Carrière, in whose academy, Matisse, Derain, Marquet and Puy had met back in 1898. They were joined in turn by Vlaminck, Braque, Dufy, Friesz and van Dongen.

The Fauves inherited their love of landscape and the open air from the Impressionists and Post-Impressionists, and the interiors popularized by the Nabis. Seurat, Signac and Cross transmitted the sheer joy of pure color and the sparkling vitality of Southern light. Van Gogh and Gauguin preceded the Fauves in their exploration of color as language, expressive force and impassioned invention.

La Rivière (1905) by Derain illustrates the period during which the artist shared a studio with Vlaminck in Chatou. This work is

BERGES DE LA SEINE À CHATOU, CA 1905. OIL ON CANVAS, 59 X 80 CM. HENRY-THOMAS DONATION, 1976.

MAURICE DE VLAMINCK

characteristic of the collaboration and exchange between the two friends. The image is constructed according to a recurring plan: a foreground of plants; a frontal depiction of the motifs revealing the energy of the brushstrokes, lines and whimsical arabesques; and the diversity of the vibrant color fields in harmonies of complementary colors which mark an increasing separation from the mimetic rendering of reality.

The staccato brushstrokes in BERGES DE LA SEINE À CHATOU (ca 1905) by Maurice de Vlaminck (1876-1958) seize the movement

PASTORALE, 1906. ON CANVAS, 46 X 55 CM.
GIRARDIN BEQUEST, 1953.

HENRI MATISSE

of the wind with the violence of a Van Gogh. The swaying branches of the seemingly uncontrollable cork oaks blend into the long, floating grasses overtaking the river bank. Here the color, spreading in decreasing waves until it expires to the right of the painting, is reinvented rather than observed by the artist: “I accentuated all the tones, I transposed [...] I was a gentle and violent barbarian.”

André Derain (1880-1954) made a number of variations of the *Phare de Collioure* (1905) during his first summer visit to the Pyrénées coast with Matisse. A breathtaking colorist, he played with oranges, ultramarine, the contrasts between the painted and unprimed canvas, touch effects and flattening. Traditional perspective was replaced by a synthetic construction of space through various colored and superimposed planes. The painter was expressing his own “nature” in lyrical form. The science of color, that “stick of dynamite” and the new concept of light as a “negation of shadows, a whole world of brightness” were to render from that moment on the expression of “the fixed, the eternal, the complex” (Derain).

In **PASTORALE** (1906), Henri Matisse (1869-1954) took up the theme of the nude and the piping shepherd, already a feature of his 1905 *La Joie de vivre.* The sinuous hillsides, overcast by the shadows of the trees, reflect the curved outlines of the bodies of the two recumbent women, composing a rhythm of arabesques. Despite the realist depiction of the Collioure landscape, in the perspective and the path forged between the mountains, the scene has been transformed into an Arcadian eclogue in ochre, yellow, pink and purple tones.

PAYSAGE AUX VACHES, 1906. OIL ON CANVAS, 50 X 61 CM.
HENRY-THOMAS DONATION, 1984.

ROBERT DELAUNAY

Robert Delaunay (1885-1941), in his PAYSAGE AUX VACHES (1906), also adopted the vibrant fragmentation of patches of color, designed to lend structure to the composition and grant it a solar quality heralding the *Rythmes* of his abstract period. This work illustrates the pointillist period of Fauvism, harking back to Neo-Impressionism and also experimented by

L'OLIVIER PRÈS DE L'ESTAQUE, 1906. OIL ON CANVAS, 50 X 61 CM.
HENRY-THOMAS DONATION, 1984.

GEORGES BRAQUE

Georges Braque (1882-1963) in his L'OLIVIER PRÈS DE L'ESTAQUE (1906). The torpor of the sun-flattened landscape is evoked by the yellow and orange hues pervading the rugged aspect of the tree, the walls of the house and the stony fields leading up to the village, in tones of pinks and purples, characteristic of the artist's Fauve period.

TROIS PERSONNAGES ASSIS DANS L'HERBE, 1906. OIL ON CANVAS, 38 X 55 CM. GIRARDIN BEQUEST, 1953.

ANDRÉ DERAIN

TROIS PERSONNAGES ASSIS DANS L'HERBE (1906) by André Derain (1880-1954) reveals a synthetic concept of space stemming from contrasts of complementary colors: the clear-cut shadows, the work on various tones to suggest light, the simplification of the colored zones and character depiction all evoke analogies, particularly in the allusive treatment of the faces, with African sculpture, which Vlaminck and Derain were the first to recognize.

In **L'APÉRITIF** (1908), Raoul Dufy (1877-1953) depicts the Estaque landscape where groups of revellers radiate from a central point, establishing through this movement of color dominated by pinks and greens a spatial unity that conjures up the festive scene. Fauvism adopted the themes of street life, advertising, festivities and leisure (Dufy, *Régates*, 1907), and the painters were open to technical innovations and multi-disciplinary techniques (painting, wood engraving, ceramics and sculpture) and to the diversity of all their sources of inspiration, whether they came from popular or intellectual culture, Mediterranean or Oriental. Starting in 1907, the works by Matisse, Derain, Braque, Dufy and Friesz all moved toward a synthesis of color, a constructive rigor and simplification that put into practice Cézanne's famous formula: create structure using cylinders, spheres and cones.

J.M.

BELOW
L'APÉRITIF, 1908. OIL ON CANVAS, 59 X 72.5 CM. GIRARDIN BEQUEST, 1953.

RAOUL DUFY

COLLECTION

GEORGES ROUAULT

1871-1958

Due to the generosity of Dr. Girardin, the museum owns a significant number of works by Rouault, mostly pre-1918: one hundred watercolors and paintings, three ceramics and his entire production of copper engravings, including *Les Fleurs du mal* (1927 edition) and the *Miserere* (printed between 1922 and 1927).

Rouault trained as a craftsman, with an apprenticeship in the restoration of stained glass from 1885 to 1890, before devoting himself to painting. He studied the liberal and enlightened teachings of Gustave Moreau at the School of Fine Arts between 1892 and 1895 and was his favorite student. There he learned how to handle color, flying in the face of the academic tradition which gave precedence to drawing. He came across several Fauve artists, notably Matisse, and in 1903, became one of the founding-members of the Salon d'Automne.

The museum owns a number of masterpieces from these early years that reveal his recurring themes. Beyond his own singularity of style, one senses the joint influence of Cézanne, Toulouse-Lautrec and Daumier. The intensity of expression in these watercolors and gouaches, frequently associated with pastel, technically highly complex, synthetically drawn and executed within a gamut of blues, all combine to make Rouault, who bestowed on art the role of "ardent confession," one of the first Expressionists.

À TABARİN (LE CHAHUT), 1905. WATERCOLOR AND PASTEL ON PAPER, 71 X 55 CM. GIRARDIN BEQUEST, 1953.

GEORGES ROUAULT

FİLLE, 1906. WATERCOLOR AND PASTEL ON PAPER, 71 X 55 CM. GIRARDIN BEQUEST, 1953.

CRÉPUSCULE (PAYSAGE BIBLIQUE), 1938-1939. OIL ON CANVAS, 70 X 55 CM. GIRARDIN BEQUEST, 1953.

GEORGES ROUAULT

À TABARIN (1905, shown at the Salon des Indépendants in 1906) provides a serious vision of the circus enhanced by vibrant graphic and colored notations. The distorted body of the girl in **FILLE** (1906) is steeped in blue tones, interjecting a melancholy distancing which attenuates the coarseness conveyed by the red patches of the garters and make-up.

After *Filles* and *Clowns*, Georges Rouault was able to devote a great part of his time to engraving, thanks to a contract drawn up in 1907 with the art dealer Ambroise Vollard, which provided relative material comfort. Meantime, impasto multi-layered oil painting, used exclusively after 1918, replaced watercolor. The black outlines, inspired by both stained glass and Cézanne, became increasingly structural over the years, drawing a parallel with the black and white work developed in engraving. From 1930 on, the profane figure of the clown became incarnated by Pierrot, both often identified with Christ because of the derision they inspired. Georges Rouault was himself a fervent believer, and managed to invest an intense spiritual charge into the biblical landscapes he depicted with simplicity in an endlessly reworked, intense and varied chromatism (**CRÉPUSCULE**, 1938-1939).

"Painting of joy!... And why not? I have been so fulfilled by painting, so imbued with painting, forgetting all in deep dark despair. Critics failed to notice, because my subjects were tragic. But is joy only to be found in the subject one is painting?"
(G. Rouault, introduction to *Stella vespertina*, 1947)

M.S.

CUBISM AND ITS LEGACY

The 1907 Salon d'Automne paid tribute to the late Cézanne. Henceforward, his work, along with primitive art, particularly traditional African sculpture, became the essential points of reference for early Cubism (Picasso, *Les Demoiselles d'Avignon,* 1907, MoMA, New York). This legendary work by the Spanish artist was a major new element in the fierce theoretical debate over the future of painting, concerning the composition of figures. This debate had been running through the Parisian art scene since the Salon des Indépendants, where Matisses's *Nu bleu* (1907, Baltimore Museum of Art) had been exhibited, along with Derain's first version of his *Baigneuses* (1907, MoMA, New York), which occupied the "ugly area." It overturned traditional vision and the aesthetic canons of what is beautiful, pleasurable and "pleasant," bringing them down into a new sphere of confrontation between painting and creature, supporter and creator.

In 1908, a number of former Fauvist artists (Braque, Derain, Dufy, Friesz) gathered around Picasso to form the developing Cubist movement. The word "Cubism," which was used for the first time by Louis Vauxcelles (or Matisse) during a Braque exhibition at Kahnweiler's gallery, only became more widely accepted later with Apollinaire's texts and the theoretical work of the painters Gleizes and Metzinger, which appeared in 1912. And as late as 1908, the

BAIGNEUSES, CA 1908. OIL ON CANVAS, 38 X 46 CM.
MATHILDE AMOS DONATION, 1955.

ANDRÉ DERAIN

American Gelett Burgess lumped together the French and European avant-garde artists Picasso, Derain, Braque, Matisse and Czobel, defining them all as Fauves in his article, "The wild beasts of Paris." In 1909, Braque once again exhibited his large *Nu debout* under the Fauvist banner during the second Golden Fleece Salon in Moscow.

BAIGNEUSES (ca 1908) by André Derain (1880-1954) was a sketch for the monumental version in the Prague National Gallery. It represents an essential landmark in the search for a personal interpretation of Cézannian Cubism and Primitivism, using a chromatic and thematic range similar to the painter from Aix. *L'Autumne* (1908) by Friesz, is a sketch for *L'Autumne* now in the Oslo Museum. It offers another vision on the theme of farm labor, a subject he treated according to "linear plasticity," which gave volume to the figures.

NATURE MORTE À LA TABLE, 1910. OIL ON CANVAS, 92 X 71 CM.
GIRARDIN BEQUEST, 1953.

ANDRÉ DERAIN

In the same vein, *Tête de Femme, la Pêcheuse* (1908), by Braque, does not have any hierarchy between the figure and the background. It is another of the recurring references to Cézanne that were common in the early Cubist movement and which can still be seen in the geometric rigor and pure harmony of NATURE MORTE À LA TABLE (1910) by Derain.

From 1908, the year they met, to the summer of 1914, when Picasso traveled with Braque and Derain to the Avignon train station when they were mobilized, the two artists developed the most radical and innovative phases of Cubism: decopsing the motif, inspired from a landscape (*L'Estaque,* Horta de Abro) and expanding the subjects to include objects, then human figures in the enclosed space of the studio. The works included the simultaneous vision of several angles and a light that was more abstract than observed, an almost prismatic rendering of objects with multiple facets, using a chromatic range of just browns and grays — even to the break up and fragmentation of planes, which altered perception.

In LE PIGEON AUX PETITS POIS (1911) by Pablo Picasso (1881-1973), a number of elements can still be identified — the peas,the pigeon and the flame of a candle in the center and a glass on the right — representing metaphors of reality and plastic landmarks in its disintegration through painting. The depiction of these objects and the introduction of letters do not alleviate the difficulty of its overall interpretation. The independence of the planes in relation to the volumes from which they stem, the confusion between the lines defining the forms and those limiting the planes, and the color applied in delicate touches to blur the composition are all characteristics which identify this work with “analytical Cubism.” Starting in 1912, Picasso and Braque — who had reached the limits of this analytical technique — felt the need to reintroduce “reality” into their paintings. “In other words,” wrote D.-H. Kahnweiler, “instead of imitating forms, even partially, instead of

LE VIEUX MARC, CA 1914. OIL AND SAND ON CANVAS, 38.5 X 55.5 CM. GIRARDIN BEQUEST, 1953.

PABLO PICASSO

representing several aspects of the same object, a single form was invented, in a way synthetizing the object, a sign which signified the object instead of imitating it" (*Entretiens avec Crémieux,* Gallimard, 1961). In these works of so-called "synthetic" Cubism, the canvas took on a conceptual unity, with the essential signs and fragments of reality: sand, newspapers, wallpaper and imitation wood. These fragments provided an opportunity of reintroducing color and varying the textures.

Using the simplified typography of the *Journal,* Pablo Picasso introduced an element of craftwork into LE VIEUX MARC (ca 1914), allowing the trace-mark of the letters, before they become partially filled with color, to remain visible. The execution may be well suited to the elements depicted (bread, ham, bottle) but it is in deliberate contrast to the extreme subtlety displayed through other objects. The tablecloth, for instance, shows a highly worked

LE PIGEON AUX PETITS POIS, 1911. OIL ON CANVAS, 64 X 53 CM.
GIRARDIN BEQUEST, 1953.

PABLO PICASSO

LE LİVRE, 1913. OIL AND PASTED PAPER ON CANVAS, 41 X 34 CM. HENRY-THOMAS DONATION, 1976.

gamut of whites, sometimes mixed with sand; its perfectly ruled lines, the sweep of the fabric, worthy of a classical still life, the presence of purples, subdued reds, blues and yellows, relentlessly oppose the draft (the simply outlined modeling of the painted table) and the finished, precious style.

The painter Juan Gris (1887-1927), a friend of Picasso, was initially trained in industrial drawing. He joined the Cubists in 1912 and achieved, according to Kahnweiler, the most accomplished expression of "synthetic Cubism." LE LİVRE (1913), by Gris, was a collage made from a printed sheet of the *Bourreau du Roi.* The sheet was cut out and reinserted into a composition marked by rigorous parallel bands of blue and gray, through which the book, viewed from various angles, is restructured. This "reading" by Gris is accompanied by two glasses, common attributes in the collages of the period. Collage was one of the plastic inventions of Cubism, notably by Braque, who used manufactured paper for the first time in 1912.

In **NATURE MORTE À LA PIPE** (1914), Georges Braque (1882-1963) adopted a number of new processes specific to synthetic Cubism: sand was mixed with a range of elements in trompe-l'œil (molds, counterfeit paper, imitation wood...) and with a pointillist touch, all of which emphasized the decorative aspect of the work.
Like Picasso and Braque, the sculptor Henri Laurens (1885-1954)

NATURE MORTE À LA PIPE, 1914. OIL AND SAND ON CANVAS, 38 X 46 CM. GIRARDIN BEQUEST, 1953.

GEORGES BRAQUE

multiplied viewing angles, making the recomposition of the object work in space. In his sculpture **DANSEUSE ESPAGNOLE** (1915), an assemblage of pieces of wood, he introduces movement, discontinuity of planes and polychromy. To communicate the feel of the dance, on the one hand he plays with angles, sharp ridges and more rounded elements, and on the other traces white scallops on the wood itself to imitate lace and the flounces of the dress uplifted by the movement of the body. The sculpture pivots around a diagonal axis defining a cylindrical volume. The energy of the work provides the onlooker with an acute perception of the precarious nature of reality.

Only a few initiates — friends, artists or poets — were aware of the work by Braque and Picasso. Cubism first appeared to the public at the Salon des Indépendants in 1911. Paintings by Metzinger, Gleizes, Delauney, Léger, Le Fauconnier and La Fresnaye were exhibited in rooms 41 and 43. Both the critics and general public considered the work to be scandalous. Given the overall misunderstanding, the artists using this new Cubist vocabulary grouped together, while a large number of theoretical and critical texts were published about the movement. In 1912, Gleizes and Metzinger published *Du cubisme*, the first theoretical pamphlet devoted to the movement, to which they attributed "a certain measure of realism," for as they pointed out "one cannot suddenly praise an art form to the skies" (*Du cubisme*, Éditions Figuière, 1912, p.17). At the same time, in October of 1912, the Boétie gallery featured La Section d'Or, the first major group exhibition of artists from the 1911 Salon des Indépendants and the group of Puteaux artists (Marcel Duchamp, Duchamp Villon, Kupka, Picabia, Villon and others). Apollinaire wrote at the time of "the division of Cubism," and, in *Les Peintres Cubistes* (1913), drew up a typology stating that Cubism was a required step for every avant-garde artist. These artists replaced the static constructions of Braque

DANSEUSE ESPAGNOLE, 1915. PAINTED WOOD, 34 X 14 X 11.5 CM.
EMANUELE SARMIENTO DONATION, 1936.

HENRI LAURENS

and Picasso with simultaneity ("the fact of moving around an object in order to grasp several successive appearances which, blended into a single picture, re-create it within a timespan," *Du cubisme,* op. cit., p. 36), movement and color, confirming the motto: "to shed light is to reveal; to apply color is to specify the type of revelation" (ibid., p. 26). They paved the way for a pacified form of Cubism, sometimes lyrical and idealized, but always humanized, seeking to bring together a new history painting and the modern world.

LES BAIGNEUSES, 1912. OIL ON CANVAS, 105 X 171 CM.
GIRARDIN BEQUEST, 1953.

ALBERT GLEIZES

LES BAIGNEUSES (1912) by Gleizes (1881-1953) is a good illustration of the humanist and reconciled vision of the artist. The classical theme of the bathers was up-dated in an ambitious composition combining an agricultural and industrial landscape, with a moderate Cubist vocabulary.

L'OISEAU BLEU (1913) by Jean Metzinger (1883-1957) is described by Guillaume Apollinaire as "the most important work so far by this controversial artist. It is difficult, without prior reflection, to express in a few lines all the inventiveness and magic of this well-painted work. One can no longer say that Cubism is sad painting : it is gala painting, full of nobility, measure and daring" ("Montjoie! March 18, 1913," *Chroniques d'art,* Gallimard, 1960).

L'OISEAU BLEU, 1913. OIL ON CANVAS, 230 X 196 CM. PURCHASE, 1937.

JEAN METZINGER

ESCALE, 1913. OIL ON CANVAS, 210 X 185 CM. PURCHASE, 1937.

ANDRÉ LHOTE

Three naked women, in languid poses like the iconographic tradition of the *Judgement of Paris*, are day-dreaming. The setting, both real and imaginary (the city, Paris and the dome of the Sacré-Cœur, a boat on the ocean, a beach) is depicted in a realistic manner, whereas the figures are imbued with the teachings of Cubism. The composition is given balance by clusters of ascending lines, which are arranged around the central figure of the woman embracing the bluebird. The latter comes perhaps from Maeterlink's famous tale of the same name (1908): the bluebird brings happiness, and its quest grants the possibility of abolishing time, bringing the dead back to life and opening the gates of paradise. In the tale, there are times when the nocturnal visions take shape in the morning light, perturbing reality.

In **ESCALE** (1913), André Lhote (1885-1962) created a more prosaic picture of woman, reinterpreting the Cubist language in his own toned-down fashion. In a harbor setting, where prostitutes await the sailors coming on shore, the artist has placed two intertwined dancers in the foreground. The movement of the dance is echoed by the prostitute behind, and also, in the background, by the hint of a bustling, busy port. Here, the contemporary world and city are synonymous with energy and pleasure but also with claustrophobia. The women may be wearing figure-hugging satin dresses to emphasize their sensuality, but the bitter expression on the mouth of the woman in the pink dress and the indifference in people's eyes betrays the solitude of the characters. In this parody imbued with insinuation and fake joy, a pseudo-Mediterranean light hardens the faces.

Purism, as outlined by Ozenfant and Jeanneret (alias Le Corbusier) in the manifesto *Après le cubisme*, 1918, and developed in the magazine *L'Esprit nouveau*, 1920-1925, extended considerably the lessons of synthetic Cubism.

GRANDE NATURE MORTE (1926) by Amédée Ozenfant (1886-1966) illustrates a number of characteristics from this movement that was, however, best represented in architecture. The recurring theme is that of still life, regrouping ordinary objects in a geometrical composition, painted in a somber range. The almost mineral static quality of the work is the fulfillment of an austere quest: to find within art the "invariables" which correspond to the laws governing science, granting them the most standardized form possible. "One can create a picture like a machine. The picture is a mechanism for creating emotion" (*Après le cubisme,* Éditions des Commentaires, 1918)

J.M. and C.D.

GRANDE NATURE MORTE, 1926. OIL ON CANVAS, 330 X 300 CM.
DONATED BY THE ARTIST, 1963.

AMÉDÉE OZENFANT

LES DISQUES, 1918. ON CANVAS, 240 X 180 CM. PURCHASE, 1937.

FERNAND LÉGER

MAJOR FIGURES

FERNAND LÉGER

1881-1955

Fernand Léger studied briefly at the École des Arts Décoratifs and in the studios of the painters Gérôme and Frrrier, but then opted for painting. He discovered Cézanne at the 1904 Salon d'Automne: "Cézanne taught me to love form and volume, and inspired me to concentrate on drawing." He joined forces with Cubism without giving up color and in 1913 created the radical series "Contrastes de formes," elaborating upon the principles of his aesthetic outlook, aimed at obtaining maximum plastic intensity: "I set curves against straight lines, flat surfaces against reliefs, pure local tones against shaded grays."

He was drafted in 1914 and gave up work for three years while he was on the front line. The war proved to be a decisive experience: "I was blinded by an open 75 rifle breech in blazing sunshine...

It was more helpful to my plastic development than all the world's museums. Once I was home from the war, I continued to make use of everything I had experienced on the front." The discovery of this world of "relentless, beautiful machines" heralded his "mechanical period," one of the key works being **LES DISQUES** (1918). Above all, these disks are signs, signals, symbols. Wheels, gears, railway and road signals appear alongside cranking apparatus – the syncopated colors of the disks and the diagonals which connect them conjure up movement, within a network made up of horizontals and verticals. The violent, contrasting color, which the artist took from billboards and street posters, is another example of his fascination with modern-day life.

The human figure reappears after the war (*L'Homme à la pipe,* 1920), "not for its sentimental value" as the artist put it, "but merely for its plastic value, submitted to the geometrical order which controls machines and the urban environment."

The subject of **NATURE MORTE AU CHANDELIER** (1922) reveals Fernand Léger's renewed interest in the object during the 1920s. It also ties in with Purist themes of predilection, its theories, as outlined by Jeanneret and Ozenfant from 1918, attracting the attention of the painter. The geometrical and orthogonal flattening of the background is somewhat similar to the work of the Dutch group De Stijl, with whom he communicated from 1919

S.K.

NATURE MORTE AU CHANDELIER, 1922. OIL ON CANVAS, 116 X 80 CM. PURCHASE, 1938.

FERNAND LÉGER

MAJOR FIGURES

ROBERT DELAUNAY

1885-1941

The museum owns a representative collection of this painter's works.

At the outset of his career, Delaunay tried his hand at most of the movements in modern painting. From 1904 to 1906, therefore, he went through an Impressionist, Synthetist and Divisionnist period (*Paysage aux vaches*, 1906); carefully reading the theoreticians of color, particularly Michel Eugène Chevreul; and then flirted briefly with Fauvism.

Following his visit to the Cézanne retrospective in 1907, he turned towards Cubism, adopting an unorthodox approach termed "Orphism" by Apollinaire. In his so-called "destructive" period, he retained the Cubist method of breaking up lines and altering viewing angles, but paid particular attention to the dislocation of shape under light (the series *Villes, Saint-Séverin* and Tour Eiffel). The experiments carried out during this period came together in *La Ville de Paris* (1910-1912), a monumental canvas in which he combines themes from this “destructive” period (the city and the Eiffel tower), a reference to Le Douanier Rousseau (the Seine and the moored boat from his self-portrait *Moi-même*) and to three figures of Pompeian painting.

In 1912, during his “constructive” period, Delaunay put into practice his theories on color and light. An abstract trend can be seen in the “Fenêtres” series, although a number of fragments of reality still survive. His distancing from reality continues with *Les Formes circulaires* — discs, suns and moons — which allow him to apply the law of simultaneous contrasts described by Chevreul. “At that moment, around 1912-13, I had the idea of painting which would depend technically only on color, color contrasts, yet develop in time, being perceived simultaneously, all at once... I was playing with colors as one might express oneself in music, with a fugue in colored, fugual phrases.” (Robert Delaunay, *Cahiers*, ca 1939-1940.)

L’ÉQUIPE DE CARDIFF TROISIÈME REPRÉSENTATION (1913) marks a return to figuration. The picture is constructed like a Cubist collage, with several juxtaposed elements: rugby players from a press photograph, a Ferris wheel, the Eiffel Tower, an airplane, advertising posters (“Astra,” the name of an aeronautical construction company), the names of the artistic capitals of the time, “Paris, New York, B[erlin],” all of which share a common denominator in their energetic, aerial and “simultaneous” character: a tribute to modernity.

To put into practice this new thematic approach, also advocated by the literary avant-garde (Apollinaire, Cendrars), Delaunay thought up a new plastic language, using “color as a means of construction in light (simultaneous contrasts).” Shapes and colors are played off against each other: the central player and the Eiffel Tower, the repetition of triangles (player, tower, clouds, the letter “A”),

L'ÉQUIPE DE CARDIFF TROISIÈME REPRÉSENTATION, 1913.
OIL ON CANVAS, 326 X 208 CM. PURCHASE, 1937.

ROBERT DELAUNAY

the wheel which gives structure and rhythm to the upper part of the picture, acting virtually like a chromatic circle, and finally the yellow poster, contrasting with the blues, greens and oranges and simultaneously setting off all the colors in the solar spectrum. Apollinaire commented on the painting at the 1913 Salon des Indépendants: "The most modern canvas in the whole Salon. There is nothing derivative about this painting, vibrating not only with the contrast of complementaries as discovered by Seurat but in which each hue evokes and becomes suffused with all the other colors of the prism. This is simultaneity" ("Montjoie! March 18, 1913." *Chroniques d'art*, Gallimard, 1960.)

The synthesis between the eulogy of a modern subject and Orphism comes to fruition in the watercolor from the Henry-Thomas donation belonging to the series HOMMAGE À BLÉRIOT (1914). The Blériot airplane, like the Eiffel Tower and the Voisin biplane, borrowed from *L'Équipe de Cardiff*, blends with the colored circles of the rotating propellers and cockades. Due to its circular forms, the report of the event – the Channel crossing – dwindles in the face of the description of the "movement of light" (Sonia Delaunay).

Femme nue lisant and SYMPHONIE COLORÉE or *Nature morte portugaise* (1915-1916) were painted in Spain and Portugal during the war, and sprang from the violent contrast of light and color. Again Delaunay combined real elements with circular forms – fruit, plants, a hat and decorative patterns. In 1926, Delaunay returned to the theme of the Eiffel Tower as a background for portraits or as a subject in its own right. In *Tour Eiffel* (1926), from the Henry-Thomas donation, for instance, an aerial view of the monument gives it a dizzying perspective, in a synthetic approach to forms and colors

D.G.

HOMMAGE À BLÉRIOT, 1914. WATERCOLOR MOUNTED ON PAPER, 78 X 67 CM. HENRY-THOMAS DONATION, 1976.

ROBERT DELAUNAY

NATURE MORTE PORTUGAISE OU SYMPHONIE COLORÉE, 1915-1916.
OIL ON CANVAS, 144 X 204 CM. GIRARDIN BEQUEST, 1953.

ROBERT DELAUNAY

DADA AND SURREALISM

DADA

The collection has very few Dada or Surrealist works, as they have rarely been included in major donations and were not formerly purchased by the museum. An initial, small core formed by Jean Crotti's unique works and a small number of paintings by Picabia, De Chirico and Max Ernst, grew with the acquisition of two works by Kurt Schwitters and the considerable Victor Brauner bequest. More recently, the museum added to the Francis Picabia collection and formed a set of editions by Marcel Duchamp, while pursuing acquisitions of Surrealist photographs.

Dada – or Dadaism – first appeared in Zurich (through the German Hugo Ball, the Swiss Richard Hülsenbeck, the Romanians Tristan Tzara and Marcel Janco and the Alsacian Hans Arp). The term was coined there in 1916, in an anti-war climate, while in New York another center was developing around Marcel Duchamp and Francis Picabia, who had arrived in 1915. After the war, Dada spread just about everywhere: to Berlin (Richard Hülsenbeck, Johannes Baader, George Grosz, Raoul Hausmann, John Heartfield and Hannah Höch); to Cologne (Max Ernst, Johannes Baargeld, Hans Arp); to Hanover (Kurt Schwitters); and to Paris (Tristan Tzara, André Breton, Philippe Soupault and Louis Aragon).

Dada claimed to be "negative, ephemeral, illogical and pointless." It was characterized by a perpetual spirit of revolt against all traditional forms of art and thought, including morality, politics, literature and the plastic arts. All aspects of plastic arts were questioned and renewed – the techniques (collage, photomontage), materials (use of rubbish) and composition (the intervention of chance).

MIROIR-COLLAGE, CA 1920-1922.OIL, PLASTER AND COLLAGE OF VARIOUS OBJECTS ON A MIRROR, 28.5 X 11 CM. DONATED BY M. AND MME. CHRISTOPHE TZARA, 1988.

KURT SCHWITTERS

MIROIR-COLLAGE (ca 1920-1922) is an abstract collage called "Merzbilder," a name Kurt Schwitters gave (1887-1948) to his collages and his entire literary (phonetic poems) and pictorial output in 1919. *Miroir-collage* was framed by Tristan Tzara, who owned the work, and was donated to the museum in 1988 by his family (Marie-Thérèse and Christophe Tzara). It is made up of junk – wood, metal, cardboard, a button, metal, cork, broken ceramic – solidified with plaster on a narrow mirror. The mirror-collage was reputed to be a present for his friend, the German artist Hannah Höch.

P.75

SERPENTINS 1, 1918-1919. INDIA INK, GRAPHITE, GOLD AND SILVER PAINT, 83 X 63 CM. PURCHASE, 2000.

FRANCIS PICABIA

After his experience with Dada in New York, Francis Picabia (1879-1953) met Tzara in Switerland and established the essential link for Dada's spread to Paris; indeed, he was one of the key figures. The acquisition in 2000 of SERPENTINS 1 (Lausanne, 1918-1919) illustrates this period through an important Machinist-style work. After his spectacular break with Dada (1921) and tentative contacts with the budding Surrealist movement, Picabia left Paris and moved to the Côte d'Azur. He painted LES AMOUREUX (APRÈS LA PLUIE) (ca 1925), part of a series of works that were painted (and often, as is the case here, repainted) with Ripolin, a type of house paint. These were the collages (*Vase de fleurs*, donated by Henry-Thomas), the isolated figures of the "Monsters" and couples embracing in the "Kisses,"

LES AMOUREUX (APRÈS LA PLUIE), CA 1925, RIPOLIN ON CANVAS, 116 X 115 CM. FORMER ANDRÉ BRETON COLLECTION. PURCHASE, 2003.

FRANCIS PICABIA

borrowed from the imagery of popular postcards. These are more than just parodies: Picabia combined a conventional subject with an industrial medium (Ripolin paint), refuting the painter's traditional techniques. Hence, *Les Amoureux* can be viewed both as a Dadaist negation ("I don't care, I couldn't care less about the bourgeois and artists," Picabia wrote in 1923) and as an affirmation of the possibilities of painting and the pleasure of returning to his brushes, as he expressed to Jacques Doucet in February of 1926.)

André Breton purchased this work, along with *Serpentins I*, during the famous 1926 sale of "Paintings, watercolors and drawings by Francis Picabia belonging to Marcel Duchamp."

Marcel Duchamp (1887-1968), a leading artist in the Dada movement in New York and Paris, initiated a number of approaches that continue to influence artistic movements to this day.

Man Ray photographed **LA TONSURE**, a portrait of Duchamp with a shooting star haircut. It reflects both the Dadaist sense of play as much as it prefigured body art.

In 1934, Duchamp published facsimiles of notes for the *Grand Verre* in *La Mariée mise à nue par ses célibataires même* (*La Boîte verte*; a copy of which is in the collection). The following year, Duchamp designed **LA BOÎTE-EN-VALISE** to hold reproductions, photographs and miniature objects of all his works, forming a portable museum of artwork. Starting in 1936, he made successive series of these boxes over time; the museum's box comes from the final and most complete series.

Duchamp went along with Surrealism without actually being a member of the group, and his participation lay somewhere at the edges of the artistic art. He hung the works acting as a "Générateur arbitre" at the Exposition Internationale de Surréalisme in Paris, in 1938, conceiving notably the coal bags on the ceilings, and dressed one of the mannequins. Photographs by Raoul Ubac in the collection illustrate this event. Duchamp was also a graphic artist, and the museum has several of his works, notably the covers he designed for several exhibition catalogues: First Papers of Surrealism (New York, 1942) and one of the luxury copes of Surréalisme en 1947, featuring the illusionist breast made of painted resin, along with the inscription "Please touch."

G.A.

LA TONSURE, 1920. ORIGINAL GELATIN-SILVER PRINT FROM THE 1930S, 12.7 X 16.4 CM. FORMER ANDRÉ BRETON COLLECTION. PURCHASE, 2003

MAN RAY (MARCEL DUCHAMP)

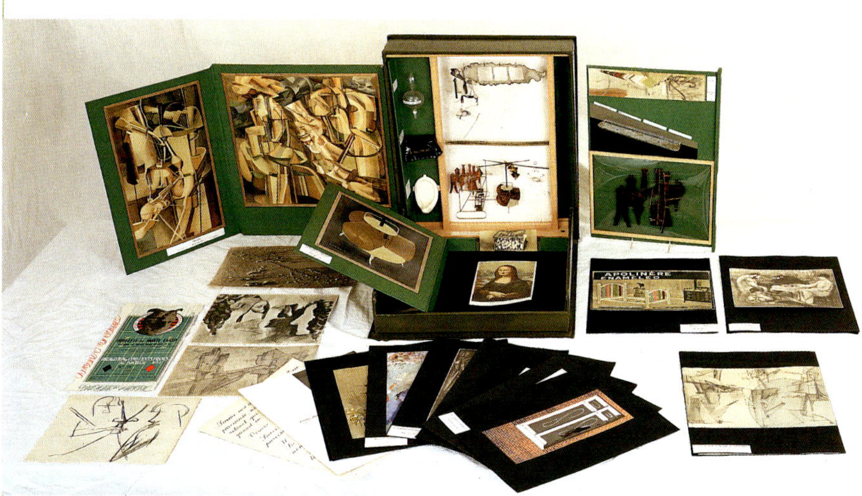

LA BOÎTE-EN-VALISE, 1936-1968. SERIES G, BOX COVERED IN LEATHER CONTAINING 80 DOCUMENTS, PHOTOGRAPHS AND OBJECTS, 40 X 37.5 X 8.2 CM. PURCHASE, 2002

MARCEL DUCHAMP

MÉLANCOLIE HERMÉTIQUE, 1919. OIL ON CANVAS, 62 X 49.5 CM. MATHILDE AMOS DONATION, 1955.

GIORGIO DE CHIRICO

SURREALISM

The *Surrealist Manifesto,* written by Breton and published in 1924, outlined its aims: "Purely psychic automatism through which we intend to give mental expression to the actual mechanism of thought, either verbally, in writing, or in any other fashion. Dictation of thought in the absence of any control imposed by reason, beyond any aesthetic or moral preoccupation." The plastic manifestations of Surrealism were highly diverse, ranging from automatic writing and the intervention of chance (Max Ernst or André Masson), to the pictorially dream-like creations of the illusionist painters, the "dream tracers" Dali or Magritte, but which actually originated with Giorgio De Chirico (1888-1978).

The latter considerably influenced the Surrealist painters, yet he never belonged to their movement. In the works created between 1910 and 1920, the fact of placing totally disparate but meticulously depicted objects on the same plane seems to bear out Lautréamont's description of it being "as beautiful as the chance meeting of an umbrella and a sewing machine on a dissecting table." **MÉLANCOLIE HERMÉTIQUE** (1919) is one of the last paintings from the period termed "metaphysical" by Apollinaire, triggered by a revelation in Piazza San Croce in 1910: "Suddenly I got the strange feeling that I was looking at things for the first time and the composition of the picture was revealed in my mind's eye. And yet this moment remains an enigma to me, in that it is inexplicable. The term enigma also seems to fit the work which came out of it." Recurring features from this period are the presence of a statue from antiquity (here a bust of Hermes, in memory of a vision at the museum at Olympus) and the enigmatic composition made up of a juxtaposition of eccentric, disproportionate objects, viewed from an exaggerated perspective.

André Masson (1896-1987) was an active member of the Surrealist movement from its inception, particularly through his experiments in applying automatism to the pictorial field. **NU DANS UN INTÉRIEUR** (1924) is composed of arabesques and has a "biomorphic" graphic quality, set in an architectural decor inherited from Cubism (interlocking plinths, staircases and paneling).

NU DANS UN INTÉRIEUR, 1924. OIL ON CANVAS, 60 X 73 CM.
DONATED BY LA SOCIÉTÉ DES AMIS, 1985.

ANDRÉ MASSON

In 1920, Max Ernst (1891-1976) left Cologne, where he had been involved in the Dada movement, and came to Paris, at Breton's invitation. One of his crucial contributions to Surrealism was the invention of the frottage technique, perfected in 1925, with which he created the painting **FLEURS** (ca 1928-1929). This technique involved placing a sheet of paper on an embossed matrix – a plank, piece of string or coin – and then covering the surface in pencil or paint to bring out the relief. The subject of the picture therefore relies on the chance combination of gesture and material ■

S.K.

FLEURS, CA 1928-1929. OIL ON CANVAS, 65 X 81 CM.
ROBERT AZARIA BEQUEST, 1949.

MAX ERNST

SURREALIST PHOTOGRAPHY

The photography collection in the Musée d'Art Moderne de la Ville de Paris was begun in the 1980s and now includes some 2,500 images covering the entire history of this medium from the 1920s to the present. With major collections, including those of Henri Cartier-Bresson, Jean-Philippe Charbonnier, Jean Loup Sieff and Jan Saudek, the museum recently decided to concentrate on the relationship between art and photography, in contemporary art but also in the 1930s, notably through the purchase of Surrealist photographs.

André Breton's was preoccupied with a desire for "automatic" creation in art. Photography, an instantaneous form of creation, became the idealmedium, as opposed to painting, which required a certain period ofgestation. The first person to realize the "unreality contained in reality itself" and to play with the experimental value of photography was Man Ray. Others, including Hans Bellmer, Brassaï, Claude Cahun, and Raoul Ubac, followed.

Claude Cahun (Lucie Schwob, 1894-1954) began to participate in the movement in 1929. She was a poet, author, photographer and militant. She was extremely introverted and narcissistic, traits that were primarily expressed through androgynous self-portraits. She explained her quest for identity: "Under this mask, another mask; I will never finish removing all these faces." She constantly disguised and staged herself in spectacular poses, with her hair died or even shaved. The museum has been gradually forming a significant collection of her works since 1995, the year it held a retrospective of her images.

Brassaï (Gyula Halasz, 1899-1984) moved to Paris in 1924 and wandered around the city with André Kertész. At the time, he worked as a photojournalist. In 1930, he began to photograph the "latent and ephemeral enchantment harbored in the streets, the walls." André Breton considered his images to be Surrealistic because, in his words, they revealed Paris as "ghostly, unreal, drowning in darkness and fog." For Brassaï, on the other hand, the Surrealism of his photographs "was nothing more than reality made to look like fantasy through vision." Le Musée d'Art Moderne de la Ville de Paris acquired an interesting collection of Brassaï prints in the 1980s, which was then completed by a gift from the artist. More recently, and thanks to the generosity of Aube Elléouët, the collection acquired an image representative of the "convulsive beauty": LA MAISON QUE J'HABITE, MA VIE, CE QUE J'ÉCRIS.

STUDIES FOR A KEEPSAKE, CA 1925. FOUR BLACK AND WHITE VINTAGE PHOTOGRAPHS MOUNTED ON CARDBOARD, GELATIN-SILVER PRINT, 14 X 45 CM. PURCHASE, 2003.

LUCIE SCHOWB, KNOWN AS CLAUDE CAHUN

LA MAISON QUE J'HABITE, MA VIE, CE QUE J'ÉCRIS, CA 1934.
ORIGINAL VINTAGE GELATIN-SILVER PRINT, 13.1 X 23.4 CM.
GIFT FROM AUBE BRETON-ELLÉOUËT WITH OONA ELLÉOUËT, 2003.

GYULA HALASZ, KNOWN AS BRASSAÏ

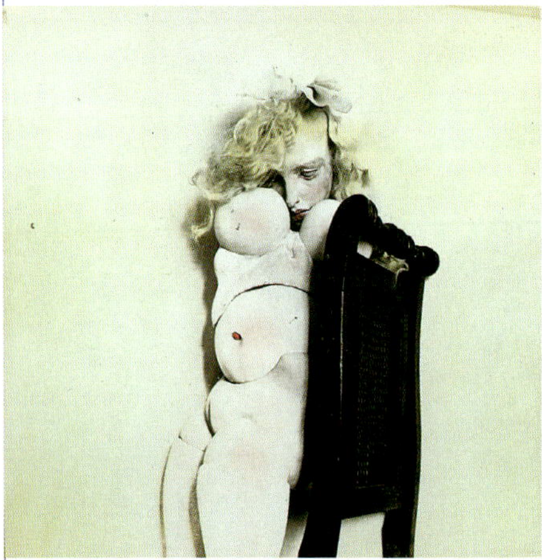

LA POUPÉE, 1938. ORIGINAL VINTAGE GELATIN-SILVER PRINT WITH THE APPLICATION OF ANILINE DYES, 23.8 X 24 CM. PURCHASED AT AUCTION, 2003.

HANS BELLMER

MANNEQUIN DE MARCEL DUCHAMP, EXPOSITION INTERNATIONALE DU SURRÉALISME, 1938. ORIGINAL VINTAGE GELATIN-SILVER PRINT, 23.2 X 17.2 CM. PURCHASE, 1996.

RAOUL UBAC

In 1933, Hans Bellmer (1902-1975) wanted to break free from his family milieu and "do nothing that could be useful to the state." He constructed a full-size doll, then another one in 1936, in which the articulations were replaced by balls so that the arms and legs could move in every possible direction. Two years later, he designed a book, based on fourteen poems by Paul Eluard, illustrated with photographs colored with aniline dyes. These variations on the theme of "the body desired" occupied a prominent position in Surrealist events – including the one held in Paris in 1938. The print acquired at the André Breton sale, as well as another one donated at the same time by his heir Aube Elléouët, are exceptional in terms of format and demonstrate the artist's brilliant technique in coloring the photographs.

Raoul Ubac (1910-1985) gave up painting for photography in 1933. He was highly influenced by Man Ray and used a solarization technique in his work. He also invented two new Surrealist techniques: "burning" and "petrification," which are types of photographic "automatic writing." In 1938, he photographed the mannequins at the Exposition internationale du Surréalisme, as well as the ceiling created by Marcel Duchamp for the event. These photographs are now in the museum collection ■

E.E.

COLLECTION

JEAN CROTTI 1878-1958

The Crotti collection of the Musée d'Art Moderne de la Ville de Paris is made up of seventeen paintings, three gouaches and one collage, mainly drawn from the Suzanne Duchamp-Crotti bequest (1965), after a selection made by Marcel Duchamp.

Jean Crotti was born in Fribourg but moved to Paris in 1901, where he explored a number of different schools – Fauvism and Cubism – and around 1911-1912, he adapted them into a new Orphic style (*La Partie de thé*, 1914).

The war drove him to New York from 1915 to 1921. It was there that he became close friends with Marcel Duchamp (he married his sister, also a painter, in 1919) and with Francis Picabia. Crotti was later to describe the year 1915-1916 as his "second birth by autoprocreation and self-delivery, with no umbilical cord." He went on to develop his own mecanomorphic style (*Virginité en déplacement*, 1916; *La Mariée dévissée*, 1921). "By the time he tackled this, he had already ceased believing in salvation through form. To his eyes, the machine represents . . . a pure metaphor. The painter proceeds through analogy and association of ideas" (*in* Waldemar-George, *Jean Crotti*, 1930).

His unique contribution to the spirit of Dadaism is demonstrated in his constructions. **THE CLOWN** (1916), a collage on glass, combines color and light in a translucency that resembles the art of stained glass. The mystery of this work prefigures the mysticism that appeared in his later cosmic abstractions. With it, Jean Crotti created his most personal and enigmatic work (an offbeat "religiosity," in which the glass eye that would become his emblem can also been seen as the divine eye). It is also the closest to Marcel Duchamp's great work, *La Mariée mise à nu par ses célibataires, même* (1915-1923).

Tabu came from a revelation: "Tabu I am definitely now 10 pm February 12 1921 Vienna Austria in black street hole. Light flash apparition." Tabu, a tentative movement, was linked to the breakdown of Dada. The use of the blatant advertising technique of the tract frequently used by Dada (seen below *Explicatif Manifeste Tabu*, 1921), and its intangible, therefore taboo religious content, are the reflection of the fundamental ambivalence of Jean Crotti's work as a whole

M.S.

LE CLOWN, 1916. COLLAGE ON GLASS,
37 X 25 CM. SUZANNE DUCHAMP-CROTTI BEQUEST, 1965.

PORTRAIT D'ANDRÉ BRETON, 1934. OIL ON CANVAS, 61 X 50 CM.
GIFT FROM AUBE BRETON-ELLÉOUËT WITH HER DAUGHTER OONA ELLÉOUËT, 2003

VICTOR BRAUNER

COLLECTION

VICTOR BRAUNER

1903-1966

Apart from the series *Conglomeros* (painting, sculpture and a set of fifty-one drawings), the museum owns twenty-nine paintings by the artist, thanks to a bequest by Mrs. Victor Brauner in 1988. The gift in 2003 of **PORTRAIT D'ANDRÉ BRETON** (1934) from Aube Breton-Elléouët and her daughter Oona Elléouët, completed this collection.

Victor Brauner arrived in Paris from Romania in 1930, and joined the Surrealist movement in 1932 through Yves Tanguy, who introduced him to André Breton. In 1934, Victor Brauner's first one-man exhibition was held at the Galerie Pierre; André Bréton wrote the preface for the catalogue. He probably painted Bréton's portrait, as well as those of René Char and Benjamin Péret, for this event. These unfinished works are also in the museum's collection.

The **CONGLOMEROS** (1945) — a hybrid being with one head and three bodies, two of them masculine — is characteristic of his imaginary, obsessive and primitive universe, peopled with strange beings. According to Brauner, the Conglomeros was "born on July 23, 1941 at midnight in Saint-Féliu-d'Armont, Pyrénées orientales, France." "Conglomeros, anonymous of the plural, your solitude is greater, body image of the multiple," stated the artist.

LA RENCONTRE DU 2 BIS RUE PERREL (1946) is the ultimate Surrealist image, an objective fluke or unusual meeting, as advocated by André Breton in his *Surrealist Manifesto.* Brauner actually put together two pictorial realities in this work: *La Charmeuse de serpent* (1907) by Le Douanier Rousseau and his own, with the figure of *Conglomeros.*

The meeting partly came about through Victor Brauner's move to Le Douanier Rousseau's studio at 2 bis, rue Perrel, in 1945. The coincidence did not escape André Breton, who encouraged Victor Brauner to make the most of it: "I always feel you should paint a great canvas, "the history of my studio," in which Rousseau's creatures rub shoulders with yours in the most unlikely attitudes... At the very least, it would be such a glorious problem to tackle, and you are the supreme person to bring about such meetings" (Letter from André Breton to Victor Brauner, New York, 1945). The "meeting" between Victor Brauner and Le Douanier Rousseau was taken even further: on the bottom right, the names of the two artists are inscribed in red. The numbers below these names recall Victor Brauner's interest in the Cabala, a doctrine that claims that the universe comes from the letters of the alphabet, each letter corresponding to a number. Finally the Conglomeros' wish to embrace the snake charmer suggests the Surrealists' affection for Le Douanier Rousseau, precursor of "Surrealism"

LA RENCONTRE DU 2 BIS RUE PERREL, 1946. OIL ON CANVAS, 85 X 105 CM.
DONATED BY LA SOCIÉTÉ DES AMIS, 1988.

VICTOR BRAUNER

CONGLOMEROS, 1945. PLASTER, 150 X 120 CM. PURCHASE, 1982.

VICTOR BRAUNER

MOVEMENTS

ABSTRACTION BETWEEN THE WARS

In the 1930s, with the Nazi regime forcing a great many artists into exile, Paris became the center of avant-garde art, and the resurgence of abstraction in particular. In 1930, Michel Seuphor launched the group Cercle et Carré, to which Van Doesburg responded with his own Art Concret group. In a desire for unity, these two groups merged into the Abstraction-Création group on February 15, 1931, in Van Doesburg's studio, in the company of Arp, Gleizes, Hélion, Herbin, Tutundjian, Valmier and Delaunay. This group was to gather over one hundred artists of various nationalities under the non-figurative banner, organizing exhibitions and publishing an annual album and monographs on artists.

RELIEF POLYCHROME (1920), by Auguste Herbin (1882-1960), belongs to the artist's first abstract phase, between Cubism and the figurative period (1922-1926). The stylization of forms could be the result of an approach to African art, whereas the decorative aspect of color evokes popular art. The wood favors simple geometrical faceting and the use of color – during the same period the futurist Depero made similar use of it for his polychrome figures. Yet Herbin differs from this humorous approach, opting for a constructive, frontal austerity which heralds the plastic alphabet he was to develop in 1943.

Frantisek Kupka (1881-1957) was born in Bohemia but settled in Paris in 1896, becoming one of the founders of Abstraction. From his initial research on the decomposition of movement and light through color, he crossed the line into non-figurative painting in the years 1908-1912. Following his landscape *Les Touches de piano* (1909) and his portrait of *Madame Kupka parmi les verticales* (1910) hc developed a series of works structuring the vertical planes and

RELİEF POLYCHROME, 1920. ASSEMBLAGE OF PAINTED WOOD, 88.5 X 69 X 15 CM. HENRY-THOMAS DONATION, 1976.

AUGUSTE HERBİN

PLANS DİAGONAUX (ORGUE SUR FOND VERT), 1925.
OIL ON CANVAS, 116.5 X 81 CM. HENRY-THOMAS DONATION, 1976.

FRANTİSEK KUPKA

their complex relationship to the diagonals. **PLANS DİAGONAUX (ORGUE SUR FOND VERT)** (1925) belongs to this series, displaying a play on both subtle chromatic harmony and rhythm, beyond the musical metaphor (the canvas is also called *Orgue sur fond vert*). Kupka used all the pictorial resources available to structure space, creating differences in touch and matter. This work precedes his rigorously constructive Abstraction-Création period and shows a spiritually imbued abstraction, often emphasizing a cosmic vision.

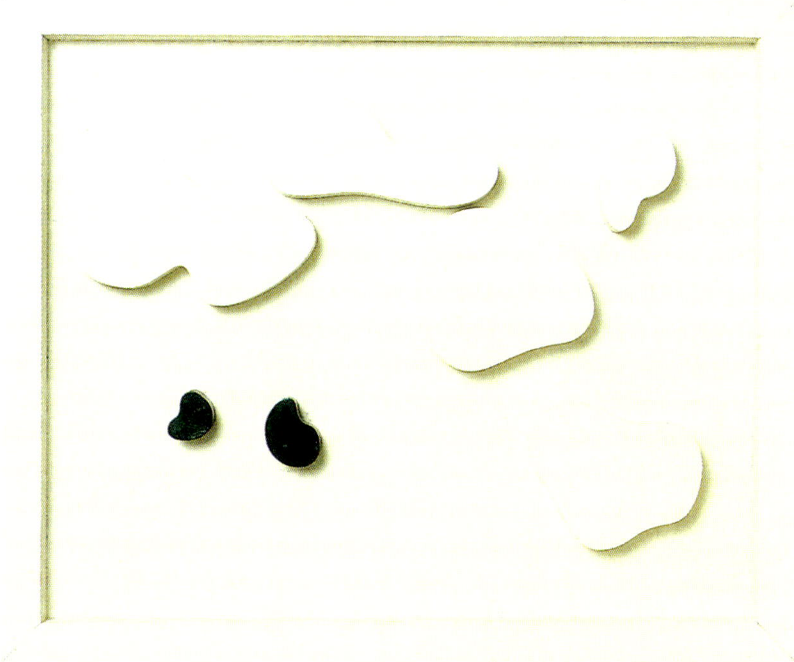

CONSTELLATION AUX CINQ FORMES BLANCHES ET AUX DEUX FORMES NOIRES, 1932.
PAINTED WOOD, 70 X 85 X 3.5 CM. PURCHASE, 1987.

JEAN ARP

Jean Arp (1887-1966), one of the pioneers of abstract art, occupies a singular and influential position at the crossroads of the movement. He came from Dada, but was as much a precursor of Miro's Surrealism in the biomorphic forms of his vocabulary as of constructive abstraction in the sparing means he used, heralding Calder. A sculpture like *Concrétion humaine* (1933), a relief like CONSTELLATION AUX CINQ FORMES BLANCHES ET AUX DEUX FORMES NOIRES (1932) – respectively executed in plaster and wood, materials which lend

FIGURE BLEUE, 1935-1936. OIL ON CANVAS, 145 X 99 CM.
DONATED BY THE JOSEPH CANTOR FOUNDATION, 1984.

JEAN HÉLION

themselves to the fluid movement of curves – display a more poetic, humorous, formally well-balanced spirit than a rigidly theoretical one. Jean Arp was to resign from Abstraction-Création in 1934.

Jean Hélion (1904-1987) stood for rigorous abstraction as a member of Art Concret, then joined Abstraction-Création as an active member of the board until 1934. This commitment runs throughout his work, his *Compositions orthogonales* (1929-1932) placing him in the wake of neo-plasticism. In **FIGURE BLEUE** (1935-1936), Hélion took a number of liberties with the principles of geometrical abstraction: first the curved lines, introduced in 1932; then the shaded forms, their relief negating the smooth surface; and most of all the provocative title "figure," used for this series of works, their situation in space ("standing," "fallen") occasionally reinforcing the anthropomorphic reference. This abstraction does not stem from figuration but marks a return to it. In 1939, Hélion reverted to figurative painting.

Joaquín Torres-García (1874-1949) left Uruguay as a young man and began his career in Barcelona. After a time in New York and then in Italy, he moved to Paris, where he lived from 1926-1932, meeting Hélion, Van Doesburg, Mondrian and Seuphor, with whom he founded Cercle et Carré, also editing its magazine. During this time he developed his constructive vocabulary. Since 1917 (in the "vibrationist" trend, a Catalan offshoot of Futurism), Torres-García had been recreating the frenzy of urban life by using grids. He attempted to maintain the presence of the concrete within abstraction and filled the constructive orthogonal pattern with signs, pictograms, symbolic elements, letters and numbers.

In 1932, he returned to Montevideo for good. **BATEAU CONSTRUCTIF ROUGE (BARCO ROJO CONSTRUCTIVO)** (1943) achieves balance through its system of representation: the shape of the boat imposes the limits of the network, inside which only the primary colors hold sway, balanced to maintain the general planar dimension of the surface.

PEINTURE NO. 320 (1937) corresponds to the stylistic maturity of Alberto Magnelli (1888-1971). The geometrical abstraction employed after 1936 is nevertheless redolent of past experiences – the lyricism of the dark-hued flattened forms goes back to the years of futurist influence, whereas the spatiality and weightlessness stem from the figurative periods, when he flirted with "metaphysical painting."

César Domela (1900-1992) came to abstraction in 1923 and the following year joined the De Stijl group. On moving to Paris in 1933, he distanced himself from neo-plasticism, taking up the option which was to mark his highly personal approach to abstraction – polychrome reliefs in which the most disparate materials introduce tactile sensation into a visual play on flexible forms (*Relief n°14*, 1937)

G.A.

BATEAU CONSTRUCTIF ROUGE (BARCO ROJO CONSTRUCTIVO), 1943.
OIL ON ISOREL BACKED WITH POLYSTYRENE, 44 X 54 CM. PURCHASE, 1988.

JOAQUÍN TORRES-GARCÍA

THE SCHOOL OF PARIS

The School of Paris, an expression invented by the critic André Warnod in 1925, does not denote any particular style, specific esthetic based on a master, or theorictical movement, but rather a group of artists of largely foreign origin who lived in Paris from the turn of the century to the Second World War. Picasso (1904) and Van Dongen (1899) worked at the Bateau-Lavoir in Montmartre, where they created the first group of artists, who then explored every of avant-garde art. Other groups formed, first in Montmartre with Pascin in 1905 and Modigliani in 1906; and then in Montparnasse, mainly in La Ruche, the Russians Zadkine and Chagall moved in 1909 and 1910 respectively, followed by Soutine and the Japanese artist Foujita in 1913.

LA FEMME À L'ÉVENTAIL (1919) is one of many portraits made by Amedeo Modigliani (1884-1920) of his companion and confidante Lunia Czechowska. The relativety shallow space suggested by a few elements of th orthogonal decor (furniture, frame) forms a background for the simplified drawing consisting of the woman's curves; this image reveals the influence of primitivism and archaism, notably through the sculpture he had done from 1911 and 1913 with Brancusi, over that of Cubism. The elongated lines of the body and lack of pupils in the model's eyes are recurrent themes in Modigliani's art. This portrait, which was completed just before the artist's death, reflects his last style: the palette is light and the art of stylization, carried to its ultimate point, emphasizes the ethereal, melancholy aspect of the model.

LA FEMME À L'ÉVENTAIL, 1919. OIL ON CANVAS, 100 X 65 CM.
GIRARDIN BEQUEST, 1953.

AMEDEO MODIGLIANI

TEMPLE OF BEAUTY, 1925. GOUACHE ON PAPER MOUNTED ON CANVAS, 124 X 150 CM. GIRARDIN BEQUEST, 1953.

JULIUS MORDECAI PINCAS KNOWN AS JULES PASCIN

The Bulgarian Jules Pascin (Julius Mordecai Pincas, 1885-1930) arrived in Paris in 1905, after spending time in Munich, where he contributed to satirical newspapers. **TEMPLE OF BEAUTY** (1925), in common with most of his works, is inspired by a place he regularly visited: it is the depiction of a brothel, half-way between caricature and allegory. Maurice Utrillo (1883-1955), another figure from the School of Paris, preferred the urban landscape, and in particular his birthplace Montmartre (*La Maison de Berlioz*, 1914), which featured with increasing success up until his death. His mother, Suzanne Valadon (1867-1938) was more concerned with the figure, treated in realistic style in an accentuated hand (*Nu à la couverture rayée*, 1922).

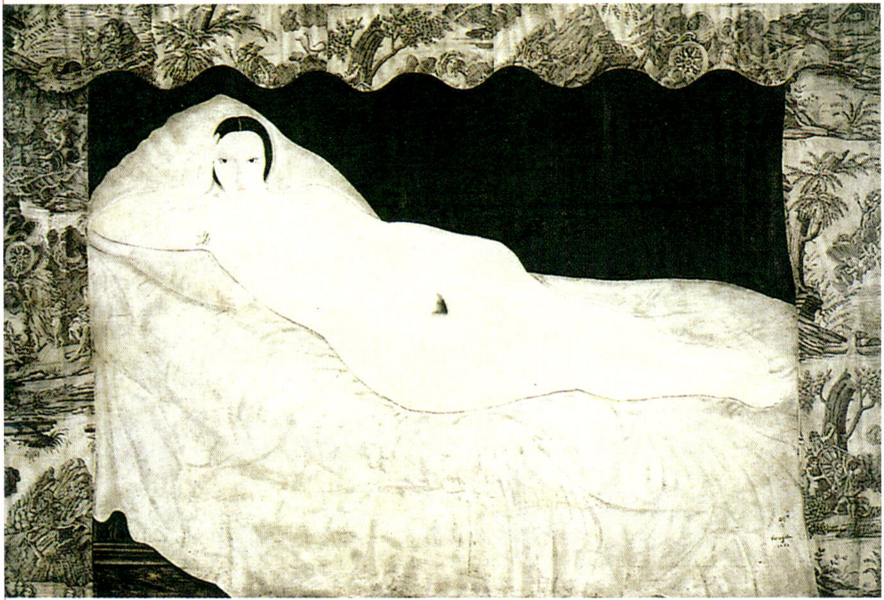

NU (NU COUCHÉ À LA TOILE DE JOUY), 1922.
OIL, INK, CHARCOAL AND PENCIL ON CANVAS, 130 X 195 CM. DONATED BY THE ARTIST, 1961.

LÉONARD FOUJITA

Foujita (1886-1968), formerly a student at the School of Fine Arts in Tokyo, was initially influenced by the work of Le Douanier Rousseau, achieving his own personal style around 1919, a blend of formal traditions from both East and West. NU (NU COUCHÉ À LA TOILE DE JOUY) (1922) is one of a series of female nudes whose sophisticated eroticism earned him considerable renown. This Japanized version of Manet's Olympia the model was Kiki stands out in elegance, virtuosity of outline and camaieu grays. The porcelain aspect of the surface of the picture, a light paste applied with a brush or pad looks somewhat like lacquer, is typical of the artist's new style.

LA FEMME EN ROUGE, CA 1923-1924. OIL ON CANVAS, 92 X 65 CM.
GIRARDIN BEQUEST, 1953

CHAÏM SOUTINE

LE SPHINX (LA FEMME AUX CHRYSANTHÈMES), CA 1925.
OIL ON CANVAS, 146 X 113 CM. DONATED BY THE ARTIST, 1927.

KEES VAN DONGEN

LE RÊVE, 1927. OIL ON CANVAS, 81 X 100 CM.
EMANUELE SARMIENTO DONATION, 1936.

MARC CHAGALL

Executed immediately after the Céret landscapes (1920) which made his name, **LA FEMME EN ROUGE** (ca 1923-1924) by Chaim Soutine (1894-1943) already bears the hallmark of his later series of "figures," created between 1923 and 1930. First, the almost gestural technique involves the entire surface of the painting in the description of the model. Then the color of the garment, a blood-red of which the painter was particularly fond (it dominates the series of *Chasseurs* and *Bœufs écorchés*), expresses the psychology of the model as much as her features. Finally the subject, where the artist reverses the conventional portrait and grasps the most insignificant, confused or tragic core of the individual. Here, the frontality and lack of depth push the figure into the foreground; the model's body is disjointed by her awkward position and distorted face, hair and hands.

Initially close to the Fauves and then to the German Expressionists, the easy success of Kees Van Dongen (1877-1968) as portrait painter of post-war Parisian society has too often masked the genuine qualities of his painting. **LE SPHINX (LA FEMME AUX CHRYSANTHÈMES)** (ca 1925) is not, as the title suggests, a simple illustration of his tongue-in-cheek comment: "I love everything that glistens, the sparkle of precious stones, shimmering fabric, beautiful and desirable women, and I make the most of all of them by painting." The enigmatic title, the vase held out into space by an invisible hand, the disquieting colors and icy stare – of fear or resignation?–of the model provide an allegorical dimension to a straightforward portrait, placed within a modern context, the meeting between a young woman and death.

LE RÊVE (1927) by Marc Chagall (1887-1985) was executed while he was working on a series of etchings commissioned by the art dealer Vollard, including one on the circus, in 1927, which was never published. Two of the artist's favorite themes appear in this painting, the circus – with the portrayal of the girl on horseback – and the couple. As is often the case with Chagall, the work is open to a number of interpretations: Hebrew (the donkey was part of the familiar bestiary in his birthplace, Vitebsk), symbolic (with the animal as a symbol of virility and the moon of fertility) or literary (a reference to Apuleius' *Golden Donkey*, William Shakespeare's *Midsummer Night's Dream* or Lewis Carroll's *Alice in Wonderland*). The range of interpretations reflect the dream-like power of this work. The reversal process, which recurs frequently with Chagall, is part of the trigger for what André Breton was to term a "total lyrical explosion."

ORPHÉE (1930) by Ossip Zadkine (1890-1967) was carved into the trunk of an elm tree during a country holiday and shows the sculptor's fondness for wood, a reminder of his Russian childhood, and his predilection for direct carving, which he and Brancusi brought back into fashion. The depiction of the artist is one of Zadkine's *leitmotivs*, with emphasis on the musician from 1920 to 1930. At this time he also introduced a neo-classical style (heavy drapes, mythological themes), redolent of European art between the wars. The influence of Cubism is clear from the almost systematic inversion of the concave and the convex, the geometrical rendition of the face sculpted in light bas-relief and the simplification of the instrument. This work marks in particular Zadkine's move toward a more flowing, lyrical style, in which movement, curves and the play on reliefs and hollows come back into their own ■

C.M. and S.K.

ORPHÉE, 1930. ELM, 290 X 95 X 60 CM. PURCHASE, 1936.

OSSIP ZADKINE

COLLECTION

MARCEL GROMAIRE

1892-1971

Thanks to the bequest from Docteur Girardin, the Musée d'Art Moderne de la Ville de Paris owns a large collection of works by Marcel Gromaire, with one hundred and sixteen works, including seventy-eight paintings, over one-tenth of the artist's output. In 1920, Maurice Girardin signed a contract with the artist, which was renewed through 1932, by which the collector had exclusive rights to the artist's production.

The works in the museum belong to his most significant and productive years and reflect the artist's main concerns. The theme of toiling, resigned humanity runs throughout his work. Monumental compositions, with cursorily depicted dark masses, give a typecast dimension to the individual, with, among others, *Le Faucheur flamand* (1924), emblematic of the rural universe, *La Rue* (1923) and *Les Buveurs de bière* (1924), portrayals of urban life.

The female nude (*Étude de nu au manteau*, 1929) is a recurring theme in Gromaire's paintings, and he stoutly defended their sensuality: "In art the nude is only despicable when it is deprived of sexuality and reduced to a purely academic exercise" (*Journal*, 1932). **LA GUERRE** (1925), which aroused comment when it first appeared at the Salon des Indépendants that same year, still remains one of the artist's most discussed works. An historical scene first of all, it upholds the artist's commitment following his wounding in the Somme in 1916 and the mental scars left by the war: "We who were decimated by gunfire, suffering strangely in our flesh and in our hearts, were at times repaid by the unquestionable presence of God at our sides" (*Journal*, 1931). The canvas is also a timeless allegory about the simplicity of the mass, pushed to the extremes of hieraticism, and the sobriety of colors, which amalgamate men, uniforms, earth and iron in a single matter ■

C.M.

LA GUERRE, 1925. OIL ON CANVAS, 130 X 96.5 CM. GIRARDIN BEQUEST, 1953.

MARCEL GROMAIRE

LE JARDIN ABANDONNÉ, 1913. OIL ON CANVAS, 155 X 170 CM. PURCHASE, 1937.

RAOUL DUFY

COLLECTION

RAOUL DUFY

1877-1953

With its 104 items (sixty-one paintings, thirty-six watercolors and drawings and seven prints), the collection of the Musée d'Art Moderne de la Ville de Paris is one of the major public collections of Raoul Dufy's work. Built around La *Fée Électricité*, it derives from a number of purchases, but essentially from donations and bequests, and is mostly due to the generosity of Dr. Girardin (1953), Mathilde Amos (1955) and Berthe Reysz (1975).

During his brief Fauve period (1906-1908, *see above*), Raoul Dufy developed his entirely personal approach to pure color, creating circular rhythms in subtle, delicate harmonies. Then, following a trip to l'Estaque with Braque, he turned his painting toward compact construction (*Paysage de Vence*, 1908). The restrained palette is still sustained; the colors juxtaposed in a tight network of long strokes emerge in a black, graphically sharp drawing with geometrical forms reminiscent of Cézanne. The rigorous construction and dark chromatic range of **LE JARDIN ABANDONNÉ** (1913) is a good illustration of Dufy's attraction to Cubism. Apollinaire wrote of the importance of this painting, exhibited at the 1913 Salon des Indépendants.

During these pre-war years, Raoul Dufy made the most of the sense of contrast between light and shade, and the harmony of mass he had experimented in the wood engravings illustrating Guillaume Apollinaire's *Bestiaire* (published by Daniel-Henry Kahnweiler in 1911), to carry out ornamental research for the designer

Paul Poiret and the silk manufacturer Bianchini-Férier, based in Lyon. Dufy always claimed that his experience as decorator had enriched his painting practice.

He continued to develop his own style after the war, particularly following a lengthy visit to Vence in 1919. The graphic quality became softer, culminating in a range of formal signs, while the color gradually freed itself of the drawing. In **TRENTE ANS OU LA VIE EN ROSE** (1931), Dufy's decorative style reached its apotheosis, in a vibrant, liberated facture composed of curves and counter-curves, imbued with Baroque excess. The picture shows a corner of the dining-room in impasse de Guelma – Dufy's home since 1911 – hung with fabrics of his own design, produced by Bianchini-Férier. The pattern and single color totally take over the pictorial field, emphasized by the title, which associates joy of painting with joie de vivre. The virtuosity of this almost monochrome effect also comes across in his way of applying the color, reminiscent of watercolor techniques in the fluidity of matter and the transparent, luminous quality of the palette on a reflecting white base.

This work is a precursor of the "tonal paintings" of the 1940s, like the multiple variations on a somewhat hedonistic series of themes (regattas, race courses, orchestras) which serve to expand the monochrome bias, with color taking on infinite spatial and luminous potential. "Just remember that in my painting there is no ground, no distance, no sky: there are colors whose relationship creates space and that is all"

M.S.

TRENTE ANS OU LA VIE EN ROSE, 1931. OIL ON CANVAS, 98 X 128 CM.
MATHILDE AMOS DONATION, 1955.

RAOUL DUFY

LE DÉJEUNER, CA 1932. OIL ON CANVAS, 68 X 84 CM. PURCHASE, 1936.

PIERRE BONNARD

MAJOR FIGURES

PIERRE BONNARD

1867-1947

Pierre Bonnard, despite his involvement in the avant-garde movements of 1890-1910 — he was a member of the Nabis among others — developed a solitary and indefinable output. He settled at Le Cannet in the southern France in 1925, and from then on built his work around a number of particular themes: still lifes, nudes and landscapes. The museum collections reflect the major part of this thematic output, which Bonnard got from his everyday surroundings, both source of inspiration and subject of metamorphosis. All the canvases show his feeling for reality and its recomposition, restored to the frontiers of the visible by the rational work on color: a pictorial and lyrical transposition of an experience filtered by memory.

LE DÉJEUNER (ca 1932) features a device much used by the artist: in the foreground, the table, upon which a vase filled with flowers is placed symmetrically to the female figure, slightly set back. From the brilliant memory of a certain morning, Bonnard has recreated an atmosphere suffused with color, and, through a play on the assonance of shades, has constructed a zone of exchange in which the figure and the background fade and blend. The artist controls the juxtaposition of colors, which absorbs shadows, from orange to yellow, red mixed with purples, blue to green, avoiding harsh conflict, and measures the dynamic and invigorating role of yellow.

P.119

Threatened with disintegration, the color-forms are revived thanks to the presence of other elements — the red teapot, the blue cup against the whiteness of the tablecloth — providing a tautness that lends balance to the picture.

NU DANS LE BAIN (NU DANS LA BAIGNOIRE) (1936) is probably the most finished of Bonnard's many variations on the theme of Marthe, his wife, at her ablutions. Within the space of the bathroom, constructed in superposed colored bands with geometrical patterns to cancel out the depth, water and light spray over the outstretched body, the tiling and the mosaic squares on the ground. The white bath, its outlines spilling into the blue-purple, becomes the receptacle for the body of Marthe turned Ophelia. The brightness of the yellows and blues is neutralized by the vibration of their complementary colors, the dulled purple and pink of the body. The celebration of flesh can therefore appear at times, through the play on color, as an evocation of its very decomposition.

The fiction of the world according to Bonnard never actually seems to have limited itself to the transmission of a moment in time and the mere play of appearances. His work, imbued with a mixture of joy and sensuality, also carries an awareness of the moment when time becomes pernicious, its recreated reality already on the brink of virtual metamorphoses

J.M.

NU DANS LE BAIN (NU DANS LA BAIGNOIRE), 1936. OIL ON CANVAS, 93 X 147 CM.
PURCHASE, 1937.

PIERRE BONNARD

ÉDOUARD VUILLARD

1868-1940

The four portraits of his friends at work, which occupied Édouard Vuillard from about 1923 until 1937, cover the traditional theme of the artist versus his work. They are a tribute both to his own vocation and to his long-standing friends, who each developed in their own directions after starting off together as young men. He made two versions, purchased by the City of Paris in 1937, the first of which, presented here under the term "sketches" (chosen by Vuillard), are extremely free in technique and demonstrate the mastery of his mature style (sketches of portraits of **PIERRE BONNARD**, *Ker-Xavier Roussel, Maurice Denis, Aristide Maillol*, 1929-1935).

Around 1890, as a reaction against Impressionism, which they considered evanescent and superficial, these artists, still very young at the time, and a number of others (Paul Ranson, Georges Lacombe, Félix Vallotton, Jan Verkade) had gathered around Paul Sérusier to inaugurate a new art form. It was initiatory in character and aimed at a simplified interpretation of nature, whose prophets they ironically proclaimed to be (*Nabis* in Hebrew), "through choice and synthesis" (Maurice Denis). The group was disbanded in 1903, coinciding with the final number of the Natanson brothers' *La Revue Blanche*.

It is significant that thirty years on, despite his function as portrait-painter to the Parisian grande bourgeoisie, Édouard Vuillard allowed himself such freedom of facture in the portraits of his doubles, sketched in their familiar working element: a vast evenly lit studio for Ker-Xavier Roussel, a garden shed for Aristide Maillol, a chapel for Maurice Denis and an ordinary apartment room for Pierre Bonnard. Driven by the desire to express ever more vividly his overall visual sensations, Vuillard paid great attention, tinged with humor, to objects and the revealing aspect of each person's working habits. This marked a return to his early intimist style. Bonnard, for instance, is examining a canvas hanging on the wall, while his faithful dachshund emerges in his master's shadow.

Vuillard continued to make frequent use of tempera painting, an old-fashioned technique he had made popular during his Nabi period, stemming from his job as set designer in a contemporary Symbolist theatre. The technical characteristics of this rapid process, which leaves no room for second thoughts, were particularly adapted to a spontaneity tempered with meditation ■

M.S.

PORTRAIT DE BONNARD, 1930-1935. DISTEMPER ON CANVAS, 114.5 X 146.5 CM. PURCHASE, 1937.

ÉDOUARD VUILLARD

COLLECTION

JEAN FAUTRIER

1898-1964

Jean Fautrier studied art in London, where he was considerably influenced by Turner. Following a promising start in the 1920s, he was forced by the economic crisis to interrupt his career. The war brought him back to painting with his series *Otages*, which made him the initiator of Informal painting, although he always denied using "meaningless" abstraction. At that time Jean Paulhan was Fautrier's main supporter. The commercial flop of the "multiple originals" (a process for works in series, 1950-1956) and the incomprehension which greeted the series of *Objets* in 1955 affected a notoriety which was nevertheless rewarded by the Venice Biennial award in 1960. Fautrier remained, however, a marginal, solitary figure. In 1964, shortly before his death, Fautrier donated fourteen paintings, twenty-five works on paper and a sculpture to the Musée d'Art Moderne de la Ville de Paris, which was in the process of preparing his retrospective. Other donations from collectors have since completed the collection.

Just after his discharge from the army, Fautrier went to the Austrian Tyrol for health reasons. There he painted **LA PROMENADE DU DIMANCHE (TYROLIENNES EN HABIT DU DIMANCHE)** (1921-1922), which marked his first participation in the Salon d'Automne, in 1922. The rendering of the drawing in touches, the subdued color highlighted by the pink of the cheeks ("alcohol and mountain air!"

joked Fautrier) are almost a caricature or a sarcastic view that is closer to the tormented realism of German New Objectivity than to the serene classicism of the "return to order" prevalent in France in the years between the wars. Fautrier, who also did not feel any affinity towards the young neo-realists (La Patellière, Gromaire...), already positioned himself with this early work as an isolated figure on the French art scene.

LA PROMENADE DU DIMANCHE (TYROLIENNES EN HABIT DU DIMANCHE), 1921-1922. OIL ON CANVAS, 81 X 100 CM. DONATED BY THE ARTIST, 1964.

JEAN FAUTRIER

LE GRAND SANGLIER NOIR, 1926. OIL ON CANVAS, 195.5 X 140.5 CM.
DONATED BY THE ARTIST, 1964.

JEAN FAUTRIER

With **LE GRAND SANGLIER NOIR** (1926), Fautrier's painting began to show the effect of the matter itself, underlined by uncompromising draftsmanship. Le *Grand Sanglier noir* is part of a series of game paintings, and one of three versions of the same subject. It belongs to what Fautrier termed his "black period" (1926-1927). It is contemporary with Soutine's *Bœuf écorché* (1925), but at the other extreme from the latter's colorism. The blackness of the hide, the background and the entrails can be seen as a reflection of Derain's influence. The muffled, inward-looking expressionism seems to stem from a French tradition that harks back to the still lives of Chardin, which Fautrier admired, rather than to the legacy of Rembrandt, whose works had disappointed him.

LA JUIVE was painted in 1943, during the executions which took place near Fautrier's home in La Vallée-aux-Loups, and is related to the series of *Otages* displayed (and dated) in 1945 at the René Drouin gallery, an exhibition which heralded the rediscovery of Fautrier. The drawing may conjure up the female form, but the matter, a thick impasto that was to become Fautrier's hallmark, conveys the drama of magma in which the body is steeped through death. This tellurism of impasto which upsets the whole image, of matter mistreating form, make Fautrier a reference for the "Informal art" that was to dominate French painting in the 1950s, under the aegis of the critic Michel Tapié. Here, as in his comments on *The Hungarian Partisans* in 1953, Fautrier is marking a militant work.

The series of *Objets*, which Fautrier had been working on since 1946, was provocative in its figurative reference by the "adoptive father" of the informal, but went unnoticed in the 1955 exhibition, at the height of the abstract movement. The vocabulary remained the same, however, and **L'ENCRIER** (1948) is a good illustration of the technique perfected by Fautrier. The plaster impasto, similar to stucco, is malleable yet retains a sharpness of drawing on the reliefs. Lashing strokes infuse the picture, constructed by a sprinkle of pastel powder or highly diluted trickle of oil paint. As a nod to the writer, *L'Encrier* was once owned by Jean Paulhan, a fervent supporter of Fautrier, along with Malraux ▪

G.A.

L'ENCRiER, 1948. OIL AND PAPER MOUNTED ON CANVAS, 34 X 41 CM.
DONATED BY RENÉ DE MONTAIGU, 1990.

JEAN FAUTRiER

LA JUIVE, 1943. OIL AND PAPER MOUNTED ON CANVAS, 73 X 115.5 CM.
DONATED BY THE ARTIST, 1966.

JEAN FAUTRIER

MOVEMENTS

FIGURATIONS, NON-FIGURATIONS

In the wake of the Second World War, the "young French painting" group was determined to rehabilitate the national artistic heritage, from Romanesque art to Cubism via Bonnard and Fauvism. This aim was already apparent in the 1941 exhibition at the Braun gallery in Paris, "Twenty young painters in the French tradition," and was later to influence a majority of artists from the second School of Paris. The controversial ethos of this group, made up of a number of French and foreign artists, or even limiting itself to foreigners living in Paris, was nevertheless different from the first in the predominance of non-figurative expressions. The latter encompassed a wide field, which included geometrical, lyrical and gestural abstraction, but also a composite style "harking back" to nature and "the world," to quote Jean Bazaine, and thus avoiding what was to him a demeaning dichotomy between figuration and abstraction.

Bazaine (1904-2001) fixed his sights on "a concrete form beyond the abstract, an all-enveloping conception of color-space that drives painting along its widest and most authentic path." His painting, *Objets du soir* (1942)—like *Joueuse de guitare* (1946) by Roger Bissière (1886-1964)—stemmed from this "French tradition," fervently defended in a palette of mellowed Fauvism in the national colors (blue, red) and in the arrangement of the flat surface of the picture into a grid which owes as much to Cubism as to Romanesque stained glass.

In the wake of Bonnard and concerned above all with the reconciliation of modern art and spirituality, Alfred Manessier (1911-1993) stood up for his Christian inspiration, although he did not limit himself to religious subjects: "The idea is to seek a language or plastic expression which manages simultaneously to retain the sensory world as emotion and the spiritual world as the ultimate revelation; to use authentically plastic means to show up the spiritual parallels between the outside world and an inner world" (*Esprit*, Paris, June 1950).

André Lanskoy (1902-1976), a representative of the move towards non-figuration – which he adopted in 1941 – developed a highly personal style distinct from groups and theories, aimed at restoring structure within the painting itself (*Composition*, 1954-1955). "A brushstroke poised upon a canvas tries to find its own form and struggles against the other forms placed on the same canvas. When this struggle ends in harmony, a world is created within the picture, which lays down its laws and chooses its own language. One must rely on the indifference of nature and trust the demands of the picture."

The work of Joseph Sima (1891-1971) is a dream-like exploration of the universe, and as such does not belong to the abstract movement, even if it is gradually pruned to the single representation of light: "Light and the unity of elements make up the subject of my painting, unity of matter is most sublimely served by light, light conceived not as a mysterious fluid illuminating objects, but as a force creating the very existence of objects." Deeply attached

TOTEM, 1963-1964. PAINTED WOOD, 151 X 21 CM. PURCHASE, 1991.

GASTON CHAÏSSAC

to his cultural and traditional roots, this Czech artist moved towards Surrealism of an informal nature, influenced by the context of the Parisian literary and artistic scene. With *Orphée* (1957), the Orphic myth of the transition from life to death as the passage from earth to light, from the real to the imaginary, becomes a metaphor for artistic creation.

Figuration reappeared straight after the war in a range of different personalities, unfettered by any form of classification. The austere "miserabilist" work of Francis Gruber (1912-1948) stood out among the realist trends. Gruber had been a friend of Giacometti's since 1938, and like him depicted the human form without artifice, in a bare setting which was often the artist's studio. His influence on Bernard Buffet (born 1928), who discovered Gruber's work in 1944, emerges in their nudes: Gruber's *Nu au gilet* (1944) and Bernard Buffet's *Nu debout* (1949) stress the primary importance of the drawing, an uncompromising black stroke which outlines things in a harsh grip and imprisons the individual in his solitude.

The participation of Gaston Chaissac (1910-1964) in the exhibition "L'art brut préféré aux arts culturels," held at the René Drouin gallery in 1949, was an unaccustomed break from his totally isolated life in Vendée, where he had settled in 1942. His work, which he himself qualified as "modern rustic painting," combines the spontaneous and rudimentary with humor. It is composed of overlapping elements, both figurative and abstract (scrap material and drawings, wallpaper and gouaches), on such varied backings as cardboard, sheet metal and wood. **TOTEM** (1963-1964) can be related to a series, begun in the late 1950s, of figures in painted wood, in which magic overlaps with the burlesque in the fantasy world of childhood.

CHAUSSÉE BOÏSEUSE, DECEMBER 1959.
PLANT MATERIAL, 46 X 55 CM. PURCHASE 2000.

JEAN DUBUFFET

CHAUSSÉE BOÏSEUSE (1959) belongs to the series of *Élements botaniques*, made by Jean Dubuffet (1901-1985) between August and December of 1959. This small group of works was created slightly before the *Matériologies*, which are assemblages of papier-mâché or silver paper. In this case, however, the paintings are made of natural materials – stems and dried leaves, pieces of bark – that were gathered, cut up and assembled before they were glued to the canvas. These small formats evoke large wooded areas. They sometime contain figures or animals; sometimes, a horizon line sets off a landscape; and occasionally, the material even covers the entire painting, becoming a topographical element, seen from above. *Chaussée boiseuse* is one such work, in which the image of a forest path can be seen in a poetic assemblage of broken and flattened wood bark.

PORTRAIT, 1962. OIL ON CANVAS, 100 X 81.5 CM.
PURCHASE, 1988.

EUGÈNE LEROY

The work of Eugène Leroy (born 1910) stands alone, and marks a renewal of the grand tradition of painting. PORTRAIT (1962) or “head” as Leroy phrased it, was a favorite theme. The aim was not to re-create a resemblance (his heads can start off as a bunch of flowers or a nude...), but “to place an object in the painting, with light in front and light behind.” The thick and dense matter, frequently reworked over several months or even years, is the scene of harmony between light (presence) and dark (absence): “Everything I have ever attempted in painting comes down to that, an attempt to reach a state almost of absence, so that the painting can really be itself” (1979)

G.F. and D.G.

ABSTRACTIONS

The post-war years witnessed a phalanx of young artists, anxious to break away from tradition by creating "another art," as Michel Tapié described it, the expression of an existential energy inseparably linking the body to the mind. "Lyrical abstraction" and its variations, action painting, informal art and tachism, were to be influenced by Surrealist automatism, phenomenology and existentialism just as much as by Oriental philosophy.

Bryen and Mathieu structured their exhibition "Imaginary" (Luxembourg gallery, 1947) around Hartung and Wols and coined the term "lyrical abstraction" to describe this as yet indeterminate grouping. Critics soon detected the influence of Pollock or the Pacific School but two articles by Mathieu, "Declaration to avant-garde American painters" (1952) and "Is the American avant-garde overrated?" (1953) put a stop to any such confusion by emphasizing the originality of the movement.

Lyrical abstraction was also distinguished from Far-Eastern calligraphy, which had achieved contemporary appeal by Michaux and Tobey and by the exhibition "Modern calligraphic painting in Japan," held at Colette Allendy's in 1952. Mathieu analyzed the situation in a conference he gave at UNESCO in 1956 on "the relationship between Far-Eastern calligraphy and non-figurative lyrical painting."

"What I enjoy is performing on the canvas," declared Hans Hartung (1904-1989). Hartung was of German origin but settled in France in

SANS TİTRE, 1946. OIL ON CANVAS
145 X 96 CM. GIRARDIN BEQUEST, 1953.

HANS HARTUNG

1935 and was one of the precursors of lyrical abstraction. His **SANS TİTRE** (1946) harks back to the works of the inter-war years in its desire to convey psychomotor energy, but breaks new ground in its tauter, more dynamic and wider gestural graphism, the color becoming more atmospheric, light and poetic. This approach, reconciling body with soul, order with freedom and control with spontaneity, immediately gained attention.

PEİNTURE, 114 X 162 CM, 16-12-1959, 1959. OIL ON CANVAS, 114 X 162 CM. PURCHASE, 1967.

PİERRE SOULAGES

Pierre Soulages (born 1919) was quick to move on from the purely gestural, which he saw as figuration of movement or even a reprehensible “psychogram.” By the middle of the 1950s, the artist had whittled down the expressive nature of linear gesture, replacing it with that of trowel in paste, thus bestowing pictoriality, weight and structural scale to the movement. A dark palette emphasizing browns and black (mat or shiny), with a depiction of depth revealing the light in the extreme background by scraping the matter, lent the works a sobriety of their own. The almost obsessive presence of black, already apparent in PEINTURE, 144 X 162 CM, 16-12-1959, recurs constantly, and from 1983 on became wholeheartedly monumental.

Henri Michaux (1899-1984) expanded his poetic horizons to include the visual, following his introduction to Jean Dubuffet in 1945. *Sans titre* (ca 1960) illustrates the originality of his plastic writings, influenced by Surrealist automatism and Chinese calligraphy. His broken, light, repetitive and rapid signs are supposed to represent the seismographic recording of psychic states, intensified at times by mescaline. “I paint as I write.../ To act as blotting-paper for the countless passages which crowd ceaselessly in on me (and on others too, I'm sure)./ To halt them for a moment or more. To demonstrate as well the rhythms of life and, if possible, the very vibrations of the soul (1959).”

“My introduction to Zen marked a turning-point in my life... The handwriting, with its upstrokes and downstrokes, is a breath of air,” declared Jean Degottex (1918-1988) in 1961. *Écriture* (1962) is a good example of an approach that sought, in a few basic signs, to formulate transcendance through self-effacement. The “almost nothing” of writing within the pictorial space heralded spiritual inhalation and uplift.

The works bequeathed to the museum by Brion Gysin (1916-1986) provide a fairly comprehensive impression of his development, from Surrealism (1935-1939) to a blend of Far-Eastern and Arab calligraphies (studied first in Korea and then in Tangiers), and then the permutation of autonomous gestural signs. The latter were replaced after 1961 by photographic vignettes laid out haphazardly on a pictorial framework created with a roller (SELF-PORTRAIT JUMPING, ca 1974). The melting-pot of cultures, blurring of language – an aim Gysin shared with William Burroughs – and quest for meaning within an order disrupted by mathematical permutations, chance and psychedelic trance, are the keys to this voyage of discovery through the worlds of painting, poetry, literature, cinema, performances and rock music.

Zao Wou-ki was born in Beijing in 1921 and arrived in Paris in 1948. He has been working ever since toward a fusion of Chinese and Western art. In 1954, his figurative painting naturally turned towards abstraction: his signs, which transfigured the elements of a landscape, were metamorphosed into ideograms reinvented from ancient Chinese characters. In 1956, the critic Michel Ragon termed Zao Wou-Ki's work "abstract landscaping," in view of its transposition of nature. As COMPOSITION (1972) shows, however, the artist was really striving to transcribe an inner landscape and release a breath of life out of nothingness.

Olivier Debré (born 1920) opted for abstraction back in 1943. During the 1950s his paste was reminiscent of the "masonry" of matter instigated by Nicolas de Stael, but following a trip to the United States (1958-1959), his art began to display new emphasis on format, color and open space, in a determined bid for balance. *Loire ocre, le soir* (1970) illustrates this desire to counterbalance a stretch of silence with peaks of power at certain points. The title of the work refers to the sensory emotion it elicits rather than to the landscape itself.

Bram van Velde occupies a special place within lyrical abstraction. His post-war works were influenced by Picasso's 1930s Expressionism and convey "the impossibility of painting," to quote his friend Samuel Beckett, rather than violence. This constraint, so seldom fulfilled, took the form of a limited, repetitive plastic range in which flaccid structures totally asphyxiate the space, transparency of color is rendered opaque through accumulation, and the fluidity of deliberate gestures is continously interrupted by reworking. To this tormented artist, the relentless depiction of the absurd became his sole means of rehabilitation.

SELF-PORTRAIT JUMPING, CA 1974. COLLAGE OF BLACK AND WHITE PHOTOGRAPH ON A BACKGROUND OF GOUACHE WITH INK-ROLLED SURFACE, 37 X 26.5 CM. BEQUEST BY THE ARTIST, 1988.

BRION GYSIN

COMPOSITION, 1972. INDIA INK ON PAPER, 58 X 46.5 CM. DONATED BY THE ARTIST, 1977.

ZAO WOU-KI

CONCEPT SPATIAL (CONCETTO SPAZIALE), ATTESE, 1959.
VINYL PAINT ON CANVAS, 167 X 127 CM. DONATED BY MME. RASINI-FONTANA, 1969

LUCIO FONTANA

In the 1930s, the sculptures of Lucio Fontana (1899-1968), whether abstract, daubed in graffiti, or naturalist, organic and matter-oriented, prefigured post-war informal art. It was "Spacialism" (1946), however – space as matter, the transgression of traditional artistic boundaries – which was to trigger his plastic experiments right up to his death. In the wake of the pierced canvases and the collages of matter came the gashed paintings seen here in CONCEPT SPATIAL (CONCETTO SPAZIALE) (1959). These deliberate, etched gestures are transformed into ambivalent signs, with absence as though perforated with matter and the presence of within and without, as the canvas spills into the abyss of space.

Simon Hantaï (born 1922), a Hungarian by birth, settled in Paris in 1942 and there encountered Surrealism. This led him to various experiments with collages, prints, cutouts, splashes, scumbling – to which he added folding in 1960 – all techniques aimed at enhancing creative freedom. At the onset of his career in Paris, the artist was haunted by the organic and visceral. Between 1954 and 1959, his painting adopted a bias towards gestural expression, with signs rendered to the point of depersonalization through folding, in 1960. This new creative method, involving painting in one or several colors on a canvas which has first been folded in different ways, is a deliberate rejection of "the privileges of talent" in favor of the unknown and "the nudity of being." This provides intermingling of motif and background, each interchangeable according to the accommodation of the eye. Folding and later crumpling revived both Pollock's all-over – total open space – and Matisse's cutouts in their different approach to drawing in color. In addition to *L'Étude*, acquired in 1969, the museum received fifteen other works in a major donation from the painter in 1998. It includes five large canvases, all dedicated to ancient art, from the Galla Placidia mausoleum to Tintoretto (*Peinture*, 1959; ...DELL'ORTO MARIALE M.D.2, 1962; A *Enguerrand Quarton*, *Meun*, 1968-1973; *Tabulas*, 1974 and 1980). It also included a second set of ten small paintings from 1950, in which "everything is already there, but neither seen nor thought," to the 1990s – like key works marking his career (*Catamurons, Panse, Meun, Blancs, Laissée*). Hantaï also donated to the museum two paintings made prior to 1960, the year "folding as a method" was developed (*Peinture*, 1949, and *Peinture*, 1959), along with a recent silkscreen (*Laissée*, 1981-1996), which entered the collection in 1999

G.F. and D.G.

...DELL'ORTO. MARİALE M.D.2, 1962. OIL ON FOLDED CANVAS
267.5 X 209 CM. DONATED BY THE ARTIST, 1998.

SİMON HANTAÏ

MONU MENTAL WORKS

LA DANSE

1931-1933

HENRİ MATİSSE

The two triptychs, **LA DANSE İNACHEVÉE** (1931) and **LA DANSE DE PARİS** (1931-1933), are two versions of the mural commissioned from Henri Matisse in 1930, by Dr. Albert C. Barnes. Albert Barnes, who owned the largest collection of Matisse's works at the time, wanted him to decorate the main gallery of his foundation in Merion, Pennsylvania. The space allotted to Matisse was limited: three lunettes in a vaulted ceiling, above three six-meter-high French windows overlooking the garden — an wide surface, set against the light and divided by two pendentives which were likely to interfere with the decor, with, furthermore, a number of exceptional canvases on the paintings rails that could not be blocked out.

Matisse chose as his aim to "translate painting into architecture, to turn the fresco into an equivalent of cement or stone"[1] and to imply "within a limited space, the idea of immensity"[2] "with the constant notion of creating a sky for the garden one sees through the French windows."[3]

The subject Matisse decided upon was dance, one of his favorite themes since 1905-1906, featured in the background of *La Joie de vivre* and taken further between 1909 and 1910 in *La Danse Chtchoukine*. Matisse, like many of his contemporaries, was very drawn to dancing, and particularly to the Ballets Russes. Two of his regular models in the 1920s, Henriette Darricarrère and Lisette Clarnète, had taken dancing lessons.

The painting, measuring 3.50 meters by 13 meters, was conceived on the spot, but executed in Nice, at 8, Rue Désiré-Niel, in a former garage rented specifically for the occasion.

Initially Matisse adopted an academic approach, with numerous drawings, grids and oil studies. Then, in April 1931, he began the rough draft of the composition in its actual format on the three canvases which were later to become *La Danse inachevée*: "This time, when I decided to make sketches on three one-meter canvases, I could not manage it. Finally, I took three five-meter canvases of the same dimensions as the wall, and one day, armed with a charcoal pencil at the end of a long bamboo stick, I started drawing the whole thing in one go. It was as though some rhythm was driving me on."[4]

The *La Joie de vivre* (1905-1906) circle contained six dancers and the Chtchoukine panel (1909-1910) five, but the one that Matisse wanted to integrate into the architecture actually numbered eight, two of them partly hidden by the pendentives. The standing figure on the left-hand panel and the one seen from the back on the central panel were taken directly from *La Joie de vivre* and *La Danse Chtchoukine*. But the circle is broken and two dancers, fallen on the ground, attempt to grasp their neighbors' hands. The introduction of the posing dancer in the central panel contributes to the overall cohesion, as though the effort required is counteracting the tension which stems from the extreme movements of the dancers, the energy of the repoussé spreading over the canvas and paving the way for the soaring leap. Matisse admitted that while he was composing *La Danse Barnes* he used to whistle the tune of the farandole he had heard at the Moulin de la Galette. The iconography of *La Danse inachevée* nevertheless relies more on the choreography of the Ballets Russes than on mere folk dancing.

LA DANSE INACHEVÉE, 1931. OIL AND CHARCOAL ON CANVAS. LEFT PANEL: 344 X 402 CM. CENTRAL PANEL: 358.2 X 499 CM. RIGHT PANEL: 344 X 398 CM. LEFT PANEL: ACCEPTED BY THE STATE IN LIEU OF TAX, 1993 LONG-TERM LOAN BY TO THE CENTRE GEORGES POMPIDOU/MUSÉE NATIONAL D'ART MODERNE / CENTRE DE CRÉATION INDUSTRIELLE. CENTRAL AND RIGHT PANELS: PURCHASED, 1993.

HENRI MATISSE

MURS DE PEINTURES, 1995, (DÉTAIL) A SERIES OF 20 DIFFERENT SIZED CANVASES, DATED 1966 TO 1977, DESIGNED AS A NEW WORK AND INSTALLED IN THE MUSEUM IN 1995. ACRYLIC PAINT ON STRIPED FABRIC, PURCHASED WITH THE PARTICIPATION OF THE SOCIÉTÉ DES AMIS, 2000.

DANIEL BUREN

The figures are athletic and the musculature emphasized. In the left-hand panel, the scale of the figures is adapted to the dimensions of the canvases, with the standing dancer tracing the curve of the lunette. In the two other panels, Matisse decided to enlarge the dancers, even if this meant breaking them up, and did not hesitate to sever arms and legs, leaving the onlooker with the task of mentally recreating the vast out-of-frame scene implied by such a composition.

The figures are oil-painted in gray against a blue background, so that they merge into the gray stone wall. Brushstroke, relief and depth effects, with a highly pictorial rendering, make this painting, despite its dimensions, a picture in the traditional sense of the term, complete with a "human element," and not an architectural painting. The force and energy which pervade it, but also its unfinished state, with traces of the artist's trials and second thoughts betraying the manufacturing process, make this an exceptional work.

In September 1931, Matisse gave up this version because of the relentless and exhausting reworking involved in perfecting the oil painting technique on a composition of such "superhuman" dimensions (the artist was then sixty-one). He began *La Danse* known as *de Paris* with a process of colored paper cutouts, which he pinned to *La Danse inachevée*. He asked a house painter to cover stacks of sheets with pink, blue, black and gray gouache. He pinned these to the canvases of *La Danse inachevée* as backing, then rectified the composition in charcoal and cut along the new outlines. His assistant then had to insert and fix new sheets of paper.

Henri Matisse had already made use of this paper cutout technique in 1920 when working on the models for the set and costumes of the ballet *Le Chant du rossignol*, but this was the first time he had used it on such a grand scale. This radically novel technique allowed him to carry out rapid alterations without having to scratch at the paint or wait for it to dry.

A series of photographs taken between the autumn of 1931 and March 1932, a typical working method of Matisse's, show the different stages of development of *La Danse de Paris*.

Following a mistake in the measurement of the pendentives (he calculated the width at 50 cm instead of 1 m), Matisse gave up *La Danse de Paris* in the spring of 1932 and in July started work on *La Danse* known as *de Merion*, using new canvases, renewing the iconography, the treatment of the figures and the composition, but retaining the identical palette of colors. "The second is not a mere replica of the first, as these different pendentives, having to cope with over twice the quantity of architectural mass, made me alter my whole composition. Even my feeling for them was different: the first is martial, the second Dionysian...[5]"

This version was placed in the Barnes Foundation in May 1933 by Henri Matisse himself.

In August 1933, Matisse returned to his composition of *La Danse de Paris*, which had remained at the draft stage, with paper cutouts pinned to the canvases of *La Danse inachevée* since the spring of 1932.

The definitive version of *La Danse de Paris* was transferred to new canvases by moving groups of sheets pasted together, by means of small adhesive strips. The color was then applied by the house painter in flat shades identical to those he had used on the paper; Matisse added a few extra touches in charcoal and reworked the outlines. The work was completed in November 1933.

The dance circle had given way to a frieze depicting six isolated dancers, with a more accentuated monumental aspect. The fragmentation of the figures is even more striking than in the preceding versions, with abruptly severed or incomplete arms and legs.
The use of colored strips, their ribbed layout in opposition to the movement of the figures, the choice of a subdued palette in order to emphasize its complementarity with the location (the

LA DANSE DE PARIS, 1931–1933. OIL ON CANVAS, LEFT PANEL: 340X387CM, CENTRAL PANEL: 355 X 498 CM, RIGHT PANEL: 333 X 391 CM. PURCHASE, 1937.

HENRI MATISSE

presence of the garden and the other works in the collection), and above all the process of paper cutouts, brought about significant progress in the integration of painting with architecture. The black compartments aim to counteract the searing light coming in through the French windows, which limits the visibility of the work.

The revolutionary paper cutout technique marks Matisse's break from craftsman-like techniques and from the intimist, naturalist works of his initial Nice period. He gave up manual execution in favor of mechanical execution carried out by another hand, a more suitable process for an architectural, rather than expressive, work. The simplification of the drawing – the anatomy is reduced to a few brushstrokes – the lack of perspective, and the deliberate evenness paved the way for the major abstract compositions and cut-out gouaches, making *La Danse de Paris* a key work.

Following the completion of *La Danse de Paris*, *La Danse inachevée* was rolled up and forgotten until it was rediscovered in 1992. It entered the museum collections in the following year, the left-hand panel through a donation from the artist's estate and the central and right-hand panels purchased by the City of Paris, joining the latter's 1937 acquisition, *La Danse de Paris* ■

J.L.

1. Henri Matisse, *Écrits et propos sur l'art*, introduced by Dominique Fourcade, Hermann, 1972, republ. 1992. "Entretien avec Dorothy Dudley," p. 140.
2. Op. cit., "Entretien avec Georges Charbonnier," p. 154.
3. Op. cit., "Entretien avec Dorothy Dudley," p. 142.
4. Op. cit., "Propos rapportés par Gaston Diehl," p. 151.
5. Op. cit., "Lettres à Alexandre Romm," p. 145.

LA FÉE ÉLECTRICITÉ

1937

RAOUL DUFY

Built by the architect Mallet-Stevens, the Palace of Light and Electricity which housed **LA FÉE ÉLECTRICITÉ** was one of the main pavilions in the "Exposition Internationale des arts et techniques dans la vie moderne," held in 1937 in Paris. Dufy was commissioned by the Compagnie Parisienne de Distribution d'Électricité (CPDE) to make the vast decoration for the electricity gallery, and was to give full scope to his technical and plastic possibilities, on a monumental scale. He had a free rein over his subject, electricity, and was limited only by the shape and measurements of the open arc wall around which the work had to fit.

Before taking on the commission, in May 1936, he reread Lucretia's lengthy poem, *De rerum natura,* which seems to cast its echo into the very heart of *La Fée Électricité*. In a way the painter seemed to put the finishing touches to the poet's work by erecting a temple to electricity, the goddess of modern times: the power station occupies a place of honor, tinged with a bluish haze and all white filigree. A flash of light shoots out, the symbol of energy and attribute of Zeus. Overhanging the composition, on the pediment of this temple of progress, the gods are watching. Their messenger, Hermes, floats between the median they inhabit and the modern world, gathering energy from one in his horn of plenty in order to disseminate it in the other, or so it appears.

La Fée Électricité was donated by Électricité de France and placed in the museum in 1964, at the far end of an oval gallery, its vast central position an immediate focus for the visitor. On either side, the composition is arranged in straightforward geometrical fashion, and relates the history of electricity on two superposed levels.

On the lower level, the frieze features portraits of philosophers, scholars and electrical engineers. The variety of costumes, postures and faces enlivens the groups, arranged in colored masses. The names underneath provide a greater sense of individuality than the facial features. Far from destroying the meticulous care taken by Dufy in making preparatory sketches for each of them, this actually proves that, by avoiding the monotony of a gallery of portraits, he managed to invent pictorial ways of merging the great names in the history of electricity into the composition as a whole. The characters are encircled by halos. One can therefore, without recourse to continuity, scan the portraits – the aspect which automatically catches the eye – and then the multiple, lush landscape, which runs all along the upper level and spans the global transformations brought about by electrical energy.

An amber light suffuses the lush, bucolic old world. When the factory enters the landscape, there is an explosion of bright red – in identical geometrically even applications, like manufactured products – representing the new, industrial and urban world of the nineteenth century, the result of Ampère and Faraday's discoveries in particular. Both men symbolize this transition from one world to the other, linking the periods of theory and practice.

LA FÉE ÉLECTRICITÉ, 1937. OIL ON PLYWOOD, 1000 X 6000 CM, 250 PANEL
EACH: 200 X 120 CM. DONATED BY ÉLECTRICITÉ DE FRANCE, 1954.

RAOUL DUFY

After Faraday, the flaps of this vast polyptych multiply and the movement increases. The geometrical landscapes follow more rapidly on one another, even overlapping once they reach the frenzied rhythm of the modern day: steel blues, nocturnal lighting, flaming yellows from the molten metal in the foundries, flat red surfaces (the hull of the *Normandie*, July 14 flags, neons), culminating in the cinema, the most recent creation of the goddess of electricity. Guided by the chronological order – with costumes to indicate the period – the viewer's eye travels from right to left, in reverse order, the two levels merging into the same waves of successive colors. This dual narrative journey, halted half-way, goes beyond the wide median space, its limits blurred by the diaphanous luminosity, to join Iris as she takes off into the light.

The fairy, colossal yet spectral, soars into the colors of the rainbow. Iris, messenger of the gods, brings to the world across the waves the last movement of the symphonic poem that transcends her. The eye is caught up in her veils before flowing with the current of this saga towards a new reading. This is a journey back to the origins, imbued with a degree of nostalgia for the golden age, against the tide of progress defended in the 1937 Exhibition

M.C.

LA FÉE ÉLECTRICITÉ, 1937 (DETAIL). OIL ON PLYWOOD.

RAOUL DUFY

RÉALITÉS NOUVELLES

1939

RYTHMES (1938) by Sonia and Robert Delaunay, *Grande Composition* (1938) by Albert Gleizes and the mural *Sans titre* (1938) by Jacques Villon illustrate a renewal of the abstract movement, linked to the return of public commissions in the 1930s. Indeed, mural art seemed the political and aesthetic answer to the dearth of art dealers and collectors affected by the economic crisis. It provided new outlets for the artists and gave avant-garde abstract art a new social and political dimension. Robert Delaunay therefore justified the social impact of his art by proclaiming in 1935: "As artist and manual worker, my revolution takes place on the walls." Following the first Salon of Mural Art, organized by the Association of Revolutionary Writers and Artists (A.E.A.R.), the government of the Popular Front awarded commissions to 464 painters and 271 sculptors in the context of the 1937 "Exposition Internationale des Arts et techniques dans la vie moderne." Robert and Sonia Delaunay designed the murals for the Railway Pavilion, and, together with Gleizes, those of the Air Palace. This cultural initiative was followed up in 1938 by financial support for mural canvases by Gleizes, Villon, Sonia and Robert Delaunay, designed to adorn the sculpture gallery of the Salon des Tuileries.

These murals featured in the "Réalités Nouvelles" exhibition (Charpentier gallery 1939) and were donated to the city of Paris. The concept behind this exhibition, which stood for non-figurative (mainly geometrical) art seen as "new realism," was instrumental in creating the first Salon des Réalités Nouvelles in 1946.

RYTHME, 1938. OIL ON CANVAS, 536 X 595 CM.
DONATED BY THE RÉALITÉS NOUVELLES, 1939.

SONIA DELAUNAY

SONIA DELAUNAY
RYTHME, 1938. OIL ON CANVAS, 536 X 595 CM.
DONATED BY THE RÉALITÉS NOUVELLES, 1939.

ROBERT DELAUNAY
RYTHME N°1, 1938. OIL ON CANVAS.
DONATED BY THE RÉALITÉS NOUVELLES, 1939.

PANAMARENKO
U-CONTROL III, 1972. PROPELLOR PLANE, 350 X 1400 CM. PURCHASE, 1992.

ROBERT DELAUNAY
L'ÉQUIPE DE CARDIFF TROISIÈME REPRÉSENTATION 1913. OIL ON CANVAS, 326 X 208 CM. PURCHASE, 1937.

GRANDE COMPOSITION, 1938. OIL ON CANVAS, 536 X 585 CM.
DONATED BY THE RÉALITÉS NOUVELLES, 1939.

ALBERT GLEIZES

The three *Rythmes* by Robert Delaunay and the one by Sonia Delaunay illustrate how close they were in their plastic expressions, totally renewing the Orphism of 1910 and after in their simplified depiction of geometrical forms, the rhythmical variation of circular or helical interweaving and in particular the radical recognition of bi-dimensional abstraction. Back in the early 1920s, Sonia Delaunay eliminated any reference to the outside world (in the context of graphic or decorative commissions). Shortly after, in 1930, Robert followed her. Together with Villon and Gleizes, they participated in the international Abstraction-Creation movement (1931-1936), which defended non-figurative art, a half-way position that was attacked by both the Surrealists and Dadas, as well as by realist artists, as part of the scathing ideological controversy.

Mural decoration was also of key importance to Albert Gleizes. This was shown as far back as 1920 in his project for Moscow Station, and also in his theoretical writings, including *La Forme et l'histoire* (1932). During the 1930s, his abstract canvases reworked the "rotation and translation of planes," inaugurated in the 1922-1923 period, by eliminating the fragmented aspect while reinforcing compositional rhythm and unity with circular lines of varying thickness. His interest in Romanesque art and the increasing influence of his Christian faith modified his abstraction and allowed religious iconography to filter through, as GRANDE COMPOSITION (1938), a *Christ en gloire.*

In the mural *Sans titre* (1938), Jacques Villon, who was also committed to the idea of modern art for all, stands out through the originality of his palette. The harmony of the pink, yellow and pale blue hues counterbalance the rigor of his composition and herald the luminous pastel tones of his 1950s works

C.M.

SİMON HANTAÏ
A ENGUERRAND QUARTON. MEUN.
1968-1973. ACRYLIC ON FOLDED CANVAS.
259 X 197 CM. DONATED BY THE ARTIST, 1998.

SIMON HANTAÏ
··· DEL PARTO. TABULA, 1975.
ACRYLIC ON FOLDED CANVAS, 255 X 320 CM.
DONATED BY THE ARTIST, 1998.

PIERRE SOULAGES
PEINTURE, 324 X 362 CM, 1986,
POLYPTIQUE G, 1986. OIL ON CANVAS,
324 X 362 CM. DONATED BY THE ARTIST, 1998.

CONTEM PORARY ART COLLEC TION

ANNETTE MESSAGER
MES PETITES EFFIGIES,
INSTALLATION 1988, STUFFED ANIMALS, FABRIC, BLACK AND WHITE PHOTOGRAPHS. DONATED BY THE ARTIST, 1989.

CHRISTIAN BOLTANSKI
COMPOSITION OCCIDENTALE,
INSTALLATION 1980, COLOR PHOTOGRAPHS, LAMPS, ELECTRICAL WIRE. PURCHASE, 1982.

CONTEMPORARY ART COLLECTION,

ORIENTATIONS

The collection of contemporary art in the Musée d'Art Moderne de la Ville de Paris really began to take shape in 1988, the year Suzanne Pagé was appointed director of the museum. Before this time, the museum had the modern art collection and just a scant representation of works by groups such as Nouveau-Réalisme, Support Surface and Nouvelle Figuration, as well as some works donated by artists, including Alechinsky, Robert Motherwell, Wolff Vostell and others.

In 1988, the museum's acquisitions policy became more focused on a threefold program, with the stated goal of encouraging a specific Parisian identity – a logical decision given the museum's status and location. Linked to this goal was a priority for Europe, with the proximity of the Musée National d'Art Moderne and its collection, which offers an international and encyclopedic overview. This policy is a continuation of the policies adopted for exhibitions presented by the ARC/département contemporain. This department offers information on national and international creation – from recognized artists to the most innovative movements – as well as on extremely diverse mediums (painting, sculpture, installations, photography, video and film).

PATRICK TOSANI
CDD VI, 1996. CIBACHROME COLOR PHOTOGRAPH
TYPE C MOUNTED ON ALUMINUM,
218 X 164 CM. DONATED BY THE ARTIST, 1998.

LOUISE BOURGEOIS
ARAIGNÉE (SPIDER), 1995. STEEL,
338 X 643 X 469 CM. DONATED BY THE SOCIÉTÉ
DES AMIS, 1995.

BERTRAND LAVIER
CRIMSON, 1986. LIQUITEX ON ALUMINUM AND COLOR PHOTOGRAPH ON ALUMINUM. 150 X 244 CM. PURCHASE, 1992.

BERNARD FRIZE
ARBITRAGE, 1987. DISPERSION AND PRIMAL ON CANVAS. 220 X 180 CM. PURCHASE, 1989.

RAYMOND HAINS
CITROËN, MOI J'AIME..., 1996. PHOTOGRAPHIC TRANSFER ON PVC. 200 X 200 CM. PURCHASE, 1999.

The acquisitions policy is based on a threefold approach:
To expand the presentation of key European and French movements since the 1960s: Fluxus, Nouveau Réalisme, Nouvelle Figuration, B.M.P.T., Support Surface, Arte Povera, Conceptual Art.

To form representative collections of major figures in contemporary art who have had exhibitions at the museum. These include Christian Boltanski, Annette Messager, Daniel Buren, Niele Toroni, Bertrand Lavier, Jean-Marc Bustamante, Bernard Frieze, Fabrice Hybert and Claude Levêque, as well as Hanne Darboven, Sigmar Polke, Gerhard Richter, Georg Baselitz, Thomas Schütte, Lucianno Fabro, Guilio Paolini, Gilbert & George, Louise Bourgeois, Panamarenko, Peter Fischli and David Weiss.

To support young artists whose works require specific arrangements. Hence, the museum acquired works by Pierre Huyghe, Philippe Parenno and Dominique Gonzalez-Foerster that were created as part of a group project, *No Ghost Just a Shell*, as well as others by Rosemarie Trockel, Gilliam Wearing, Vibeke Tandberg, Tacita Dean, etc.

In addition to these acquisitions, the contemporary collection of the Musée d'Art Moderne de la Ville de Paris also received a number of donations directly from artists, most often in conjunction with an exhibition or a purchase. In 1989, for example, the museum received Christian Boltanski's *La Réserve du Musée des Enfants* after the exhibition "History of Museums," and Nam June Paik's *Olympe de Gouges* after his one-man show. In 1995, Daniel Spoerri

DANIEL BUREN
MURS DE PEINTURES, 1995, (DETAIL, ONE WALL) A SERIES OF TWENTY DIFFERENT SIZED CANVASES, DATED 1966 TO 1977, DESIGNED AS A NEW WORK AND INSTALLED IN THE MUSEUM IN 1995. ACRYLIC PAINT ON STRIPED COTTON FABRIC, PURCHASED WITH THE PARTICIPATION OF THE SOCIÉTÉ DES AMIS, 2000.

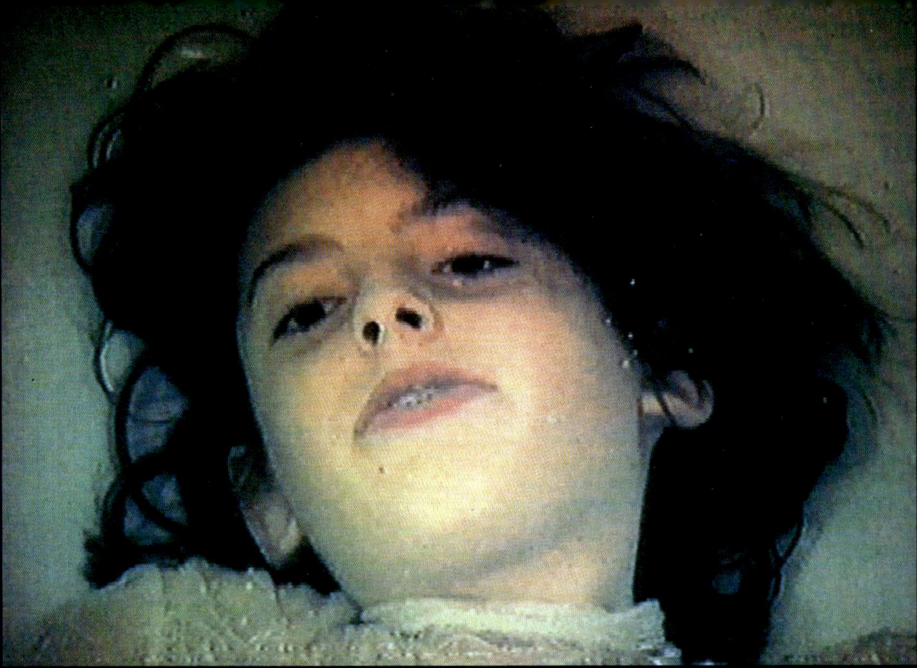

ANGE LECCIA

SABATINA, 1996 (DETAIL). VIDEOTAPE PROJECTED IN CONTINUOUS LOOP, DONATED BY THE ARTIST, 1998.

NICOLAS MOULIN

VIDERPARIS, 1998-2001 (DETAIL). VIDEOPROJECTION WITH AUDIO, RANDOM SERIES OF 50 DIGITAL PHOTOGRAMMES, PURCHASE, 2002

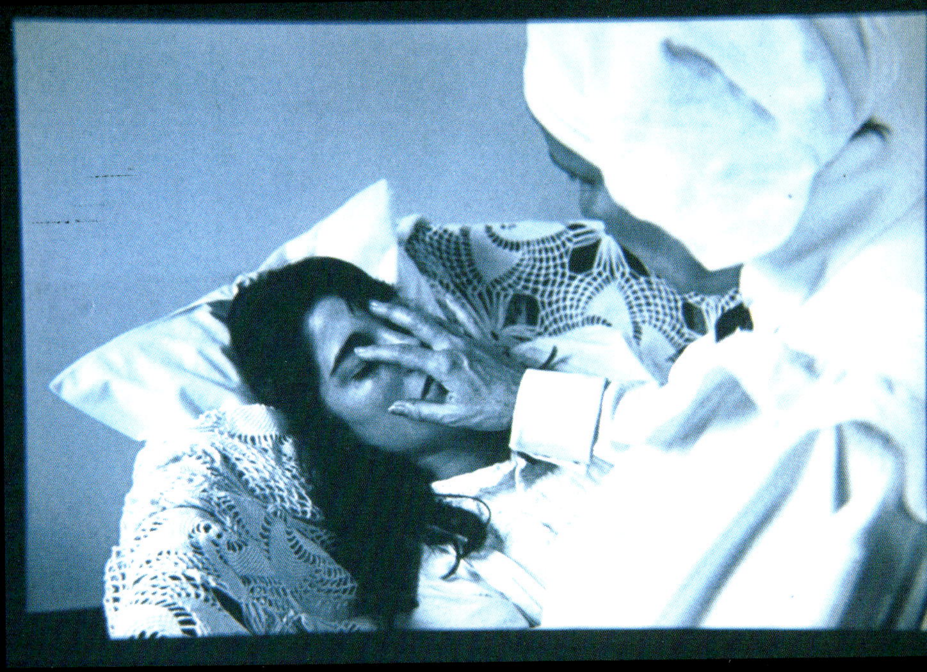

JAMES COLEMAN

SEEING FOR ONESELF, 1987-1988 (DETAIL). AUDIOVISUAL INSTALLATION, SLIDE PROJECTION.
PURCHASE, 1989

donated *L'enfant de De Chirico*; in 1997, Martine and Didier Guichard gave Arman's *Conscious Vandalism* following the "Passions Privées" exhibition; and Magdelena Abakanowicz donated the spectacular *Foule V*. In 1999, Simon Hantaï donated fifteen paintings to the museum after "La Peinture après l'Abstraction" exhibition; Claude Berri gave two works by Absalon; Marianne and Pierre Nahon, with Eric Beyersdorf, offered a major sculpture by Nam June Paik, *La Madeleine Disco*; and Pierre Soulages donated the polyptych *Peinture*.

In 2001, a four-part work by Aurélie Nemours, *Quartuor*, and two murals by Niele Toroni, *Volare*, entered the collection, along with the recent acquisition of Erró's painting *USA-USSR*. Other important donations were received from Annette Messager, Jacques Monory, Bertrand Lavier, Louise Bourgeois, Fabrice Hybert, Jean-Michel Alberola, Willy Ronis, Patrick Tosani, Ange Leccia, Georges-Tony Stoll, Artur Barrio, Louis Cane, Henri Cueco, Gérard Fromanger, Klaus Rinke, ect ■

B.P.

BERTRAND LAVIER
WALT DISNEY PRODUCTIONS 1947-2001, N°10, 2001.
PAINT ON POLYESTER RESIN, 123 X 286 X 26 CM. PURCHASE, 2001.

HERVÉ TÉLÉMAQUE
PAR LE SANG N°3, 1973. ACRYLIC ON CANVAS, 130 X 162 CM. PURCHASE, 1973.

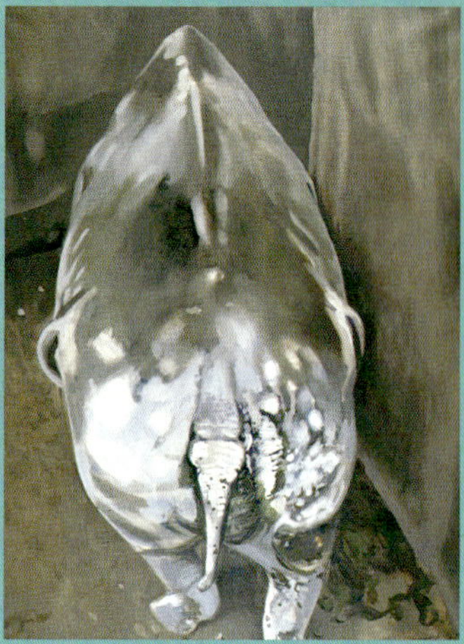

GILLES AILLAUD
RHINOCÉROS DE DOS, 1966. OIL ON CANVAS, 146 X 114 CM. PURCHASE, 2001.

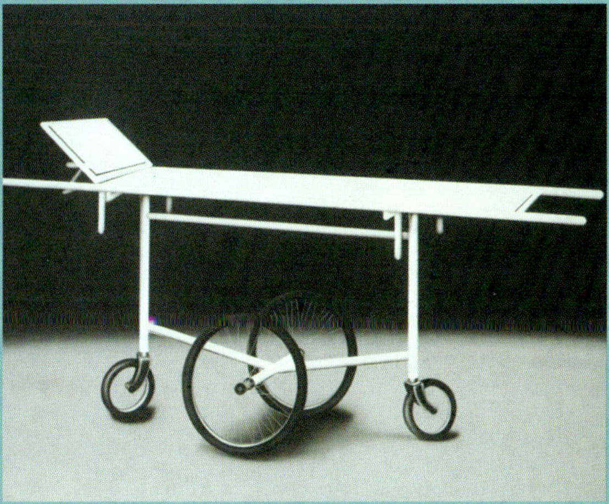

PETER KLASEN

CHARIOT, 1972. ACRYLIC ON CANVAS, 149 X 196 CM. PURCHASE, 1973.

VALERIO ADAMI

FIGURA CHE SCENDE DA UNA SEDIA IN UN INTERNO DI CAFFETERIA (FIGURE DESCENDANT D'UN SIÈGE À L'INTÉRIEUR D'UNE CAFÉTÉRIA), 1969. ACRYLIC ON CANVAS, 197 X 150 CM. PURCHASE, 1970.

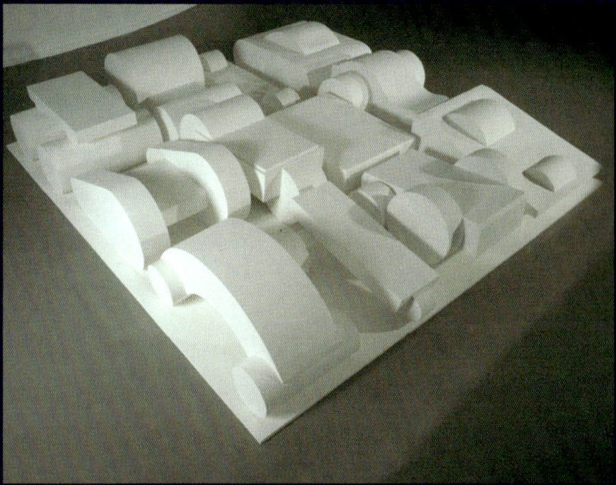

JEAN-PIERRE BERTRAND

PLAQUE DESSIN-JAUNE, 1983.
GRAPHITE ON LEMON PAPER, PLEXIGLAS AND IRON, 257 X 41.5 X 2.5 CM.
PLAQUE DESSIN-ROUGE, 1983.
PAPER, HONEY, ACRYLIC, PLEXIGLAS AND IRON, 257 X 45 X 2.5 CM. PURCHASE, 1983.

ABSALON

PROTOTYPES, 1990. INSTALLATIONS OF 12 PROTOYPES PLACED ON THE GROUND, CARDBOARD, PAINT AND FLUORESCENT TUBE, 50 X 285 X 275 CM. DONATED BY CLAUDE BERRI, 1998.

FABRİCE HYBERT

14 POF (PROTOTYPES D'OBJETS EN FONCTİONNEMENT), 1992-1996. DONATED BY THE ARTIST, 1997.

SİGMAR POLKE

SCHWARZER RİTTER (CHEVALİER NOİR), 1988. TRANSPARENT UPHOLSTERY FABRIC, DISPERSION AND VARNISH ON CANVAS, 300 X 225 CM.PURCHASE, 1989.

JEAN-MICHEL ALBEROLA

DÉRÈGLEMENT DE COMPTES, 1987-1996. (DETAIL)
VARIOUS ELEMENTS IN A DISPLAY CASE, VARIABLE DIMENSIONS, DONATED BY THE ARTIST, 1997.

NAM JUNE PAIK

OLYMPE DE GOUGES, 1989.
12 COLOR MONITORS, 1 LASER VIDEO DISK, TULLE, FABRIC FLOWERS, 300 X 200 X 50 CM. DONATED BY THE ARTIST, 1989.

ÉLISABETH BALLET

CORRIDOR, 1994. STEEL, PLASTIC STRIPS. 180 X 600 X 450 CM. PURCHASE, 1997.

CLAUDE LÉVÊQUE

SANS TITRE (ASILE), 1988. WOOD, METAL, SHAPED AND PAINTED METAL WIRE, ELECTRIC WIRE, LIGHTBULB. PURCHASE 1997.

JUDIT REIGL

HOMME JAUNE, 1967. OIL ON CANVAS, 236 X 207 CM. DONATED BY BETTY ANDERSON, 1996.

HERBERT BRANDL

SANS TITRE, 1988. DIPTYCH, OIL ON CANVAS, PANEL I: 286X130CM. PANEL I: 290 X 130 CM. PURCHASE, 1990.

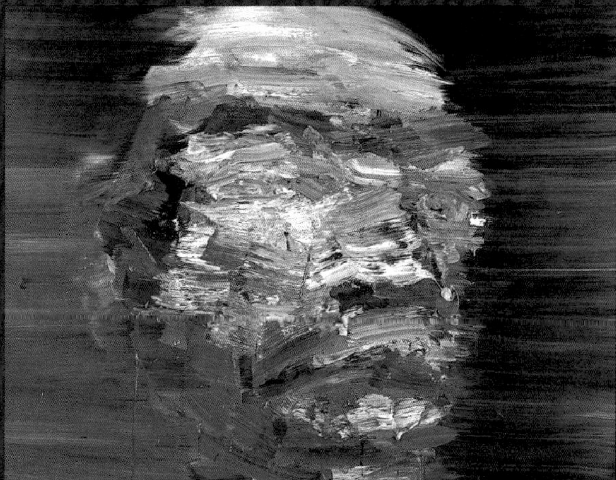

ETTORE SPALLETTI

SUPERFICIE, 1990. PIGMENTS ON WOOD, 300 X 150 CM. PURCHASE, 1994.

YANG PEI MING

INVISIBLE MAN N°1, 2000. OIL ON CANVAS, 220 X 300 CM. PURCHASE, 2001.

HANS-PETER FELDMANN

100 YEARS, 2000 (DETAIL). SERIES OF 101 PHOTOGRAPHS REPRESENTING PEOPLE BORN BETWEEN 1900 AND 2000, BLACK AND WHITE PHOTOGRAPHS, EACH FRAMED PHOTOGRAPH: 43 X 33 CM. PURCHASE, 2001.

BERND & HILLA BECHER

CHEVALEMENTS, 1965-1999. 15 BLACK AND WHITE PHOTOGRAPHS, EACH FRAMED PHOTOGRAPH: 40 X 30 CM. PURCHASE, 2002.

JAN DIBBETS
SHORTEST DAY AT MY HOUSE IN AMSTERDAM, 1970. 80 COLOR PHOTOGRAPHS. 178.8 X 215.6 CM. DONATED BY THE SOCIÉTÉ DES AMIS, 2002.

ANDREAS GURSKY
BIBLIOTHÈQUE, 1999. TYPE C COLOR PHOTOGRAPH, 200 X 360 CM. PURCHASE, 1999.

GÉRARD GASIOROWSKI
LA GUERRE DE 1974, 1973-1974 (DETAIL).
52 ELEMENTS, ACRYLIC ON CARDBOARD, VARIABLES DIMENSIONS. PURCHASE, 1983.

PIERRE BURAGLIO
MISE AU CARRÉ, 1974-1975.
ASSEMBLED FRAMES, NYLON, WHITEWASH, 192 X 121 X 3CM. PURCHASE, 1975.
FENÊTRE, 1981. WOOD, DRAWN GLASS, FROSTED GLASS, 145 X 48 CM. PURCHASE, 1982.

ERİK DİETMAN

CE QUE LES GENS DU NORD PENSENT DE CEUX DU SUD, 1980-1981. INSTALLATION. PURCHASE, 1983.

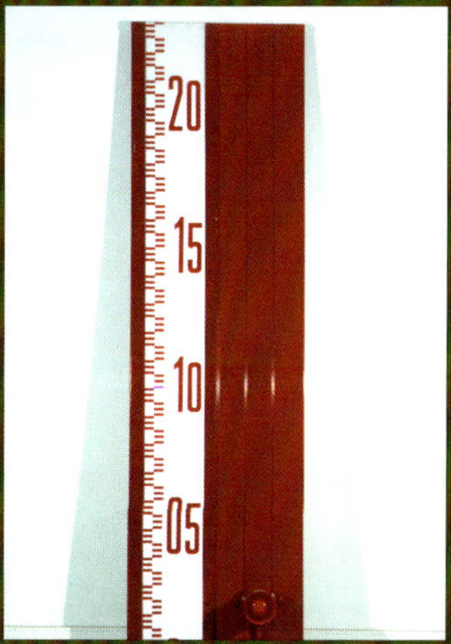

JEAN-PİERRE RAYNAUD

ÉCHELLE DE NİVEAU, 1969. PLASTIC, METAL, LAMP AND ELECTRICAL WIRE, 245 X 64 X 20 CM. DONATED BY MR AND MME PHILIPPE TURLURE, 1967.

ALAIN JACQUET

LES CYLINDRES, 1961.
INSTALLATION OF 48 CYLINDERS STACKED TWO BY TWO, OIL ON HEAVY CARDBOARD, 300 X 1000 CM.
DONATED BY THE ARTIST, 1978.

MARTIAL RAYSSE

QUATRE NÉONS POUR ALEXANDRA, 1967.
NEONS LIGHTS AND TRANSFORMER. PURCHASE, 1986.

GIUSEPPE PENONE
SOUFFLE DE FEUILLES, 1979. BRONZE AND BOXWOOD LEAVES, 250 X 300 CM. PURCHASE, 1987.

RÉMY ZAUGG
N.T., 48 D(2) MOI/JE TE/VOIS, 2000. ALUMINUM, SPRAY PAINT, SILKSCREENED LETTERS, TRANSPARENT VARNISH, 138.2 X 123.4 X 3.3 CM. PURCHASE, 2001.

ROBERT COMBAS

LA BATAİLLE DE WATERL'EAU, 1982. ACRYLIC ON CANVAS. 400 X 700 CM.
PURCHASE, 1989.

TONY CRAGG

PALETTE 1982. 30 PAINTED ELEMENTS, RECYCLED MATERIALS, 262 X 305 CM. PURCHASE, 1984.

GLORIA FRIEDMANN

KARAOKÉ, 2001. (DETAIL) ACRYLIC DIPTYCH ON PLEXIGLAS, STUFFED MACAW, EACH PANEL: 214 X 165 CM. PURCHASE, 2002.

CHRISTIAN BOLTANSKI

RÉSERVE DU MUSÉE DES ENFANTS 1, 1989. CHILDREN'S CLOTHING, METAL, LAMPS, VARIABLE DIMENSIONS. DONATED BY THE ARTIST, 1989.

INDEX FROM A TO Z

The museum's contemporary collection has been rearranged frequently since the 1960s; it is represented here as an alphabetical list of the artists.

* Artists for whom a work is reproduced

A

MAGDALENA ABAKANOWICZ*
Born in 1920 à Falenty, Poland. Lives and works in Warsaw, Poland.

MARTINE ABALLÉA
Born in 1950 in New York, United States. Lives and works in Paris, France.

ABSALON*
Born in 1964 in Ashdod, Israel. died in 1993 à Paris, France.

VALERIO ADAMI*
Born in 1935 in Bologna, Italy. Lives and works in Paris, France, and in Meina, Italy.

GILLES AILLAUD*
Born in 1928 in Paris, France. Lives and works in Paris, France.

JEAN-MICHEL ALBEROLA*
Born in 1953 in Saïda, Algeria. Lives and works in Paris, France.

PIERRE ALECHINSKY
Born in 1927 in Brussels, Belgium. Lives and works in Bougival, France.

GIOVANNI ANSELMO*
Born in 1934 in Borgofranco d'Ivrea, Italy. Lives and works in Turin, Italy.

MAGDALENA ABAKANOWICZ
LA FOULE V (CROWD V), 1995-1997. RESIN, JUTE,
27 FIGURES, EACH ONE: 155 X 60 X 32 CM. DONATED BY THE ARTIST, 1997.

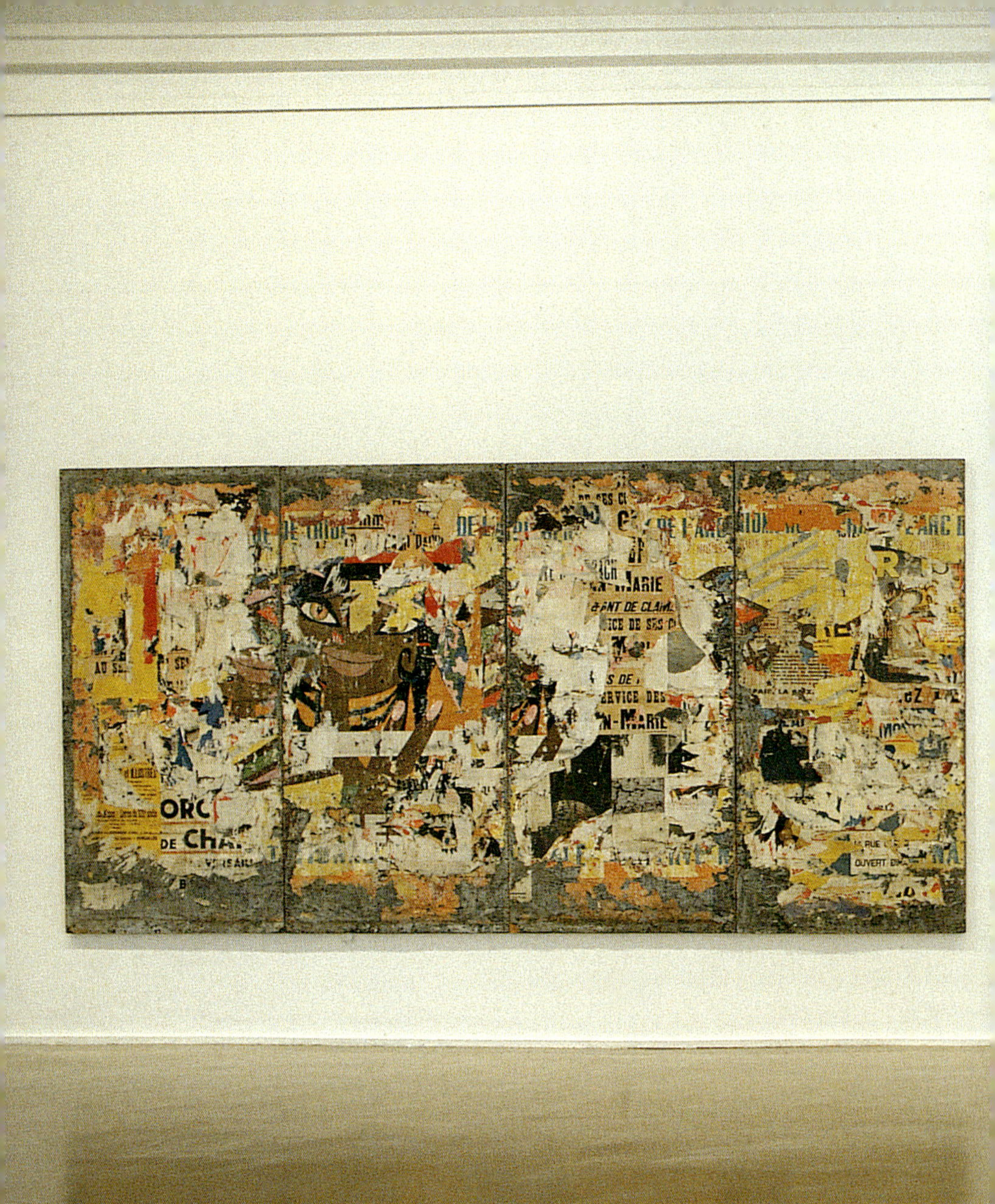

RAYMOND HAİNS

LA GİTANE, 1960–1968. SLASHED POSTERS GLUED TO CANVAS DISPLAY PANELS, 200 X 402 CM. PURCHASE, 1982.

ARMAN
LE MUREX (ACCUMULATION RENAULT N°103), 1967. ASSEMBLAGE OF WELDED CAR FENDERS. 125 X 160 X 175 CM. PURCHASE, 2000.

RAYMOND HAINS
SAFFA, 1964. PAINTED WOOD ON PYWOOD, 100 X 130 CM. PURCHASE, 2002.

GEORG BASELİTZ

AUTOPORTRAİT À LA TACHE BLEUE (SELBSPORTRÄT MİT BLAUEN FLECK), JANUARY 16-APRIL 15 1996. OIL ON CANVAS, 290 X 205 CM. DONATED BY THE SOCIÉTÉ DES AMIS, 1997.

ARMAN*

Born in 1928 in Nice, France. Lives and works in New York, United States, and in Vence, France.

JOHN ARMLEDER*

Born in 1948 in Geneva, Switzerland. Lives and works in Geneva, Switzerland.

EDUARDO ARROYO

Born in 1937 in Madrid, Spain. Lives and works in Paris, France.

ISABELLE ARTHUIS

Born in 1969 in Le Mans, France. Lives and works in Paris, France, and in Brussels, Belgium.

GENEVIÈVE ASSE

Born in 1923 in Vannes, France. Lives and works in Paris, France.

A

B

ÉLIZABETH BALLET*

Born in 1956 à Cherbourg, France. Lives and works in Paris, France.

MARTIN BARRÉ*

Born in 1924 in Nantes, France. Died in 1993 in Paris, France.

GEORG BASELITZ*

Born in Deutschbaselitz in 1938, Germany. Lives and works in Derneburg, Germany, and in Imperia, Italy.

BEN

Born in 1935 in Naples, Italy. Lives and works in Nice, France.

BERND ET HILLA BECHER*

Born in 1931 in Liegen, Germany. Born in 1934 in Postdam, Germany. They live and work in Düsseldorf, Germany.

JEAN-PIERRE BERTRAND*

Born in 1937 in Paris, France. Lives and works in Paris, France.

JAMES BISHOP

Born in 1927 in Neosho, United States. Lives and works in Châteauneuf-en-Thymerais, France.

PIERRETTE BLOCH

Born in 1928 in Paris, France. Lives and works in Paris, France.

FRANÇOIS BOISROND

Born in 1959 in Paris, France. Lives and works in Paris, France.

CHRISTIAN BOLTANSKI*

Born in 1944 in Paris, France. Lives and works in Malakoff, France.

BERNARD BORGEAUD

Born in 1945 in Paris, France. Lives and works in Saint-Maur des-Fossés, France.

JACQUES VILLEGLÉ

19.03.1965 "MOTO, AVENUE LEDRU-ROLLIN", 1965.
REMOVED POSTERS, 320 X 270 CM. PURCHASE, 1997.

CÉSAR

FACEL VEGA (ROUGE, BLANC, BLEU), 1962. STEEL,
VARIOUS MATERIALS, 153 X 85 X 65 CM. PURCHASE, 1989.

LOUISE BOURGEOIS*
Born in 1911 in Paris, France. Lives and works in New York, United States.

MARIE BOURGET
Born in 1952 in Bourgoin-Jallieu, France. Lives and works in Nice, France.

REBECCA BOURNIGAULT*
Born in 1970 in Colmar, France. Lives and works in Paris, France.

HERBERT BRANDL*
Born in 1959 in Gratz, Austria. Lives and works in Vienne, Austria.

MARCEL BROODTHAERS
Born in 1924 in Saint-Gilles, Belgium. Died in 1976 in Cologne, Germany.

MARK BRUSSE
Born 1937 in Alkmaar, Netherlands. Lives and works in Paris, France.

PIERRE BURAGLIO*
Born in 1939 in Charenton-le-Pont, France. Lives and works in Maisons-Alfort, France.

DANIEL BUREN*
Born in 1938 à Boulogne-Billancourt, France. Lives and works in Paris, France.

VICTOR BURGIN
Born in 1941 in Sheffield, United Kingdom. Lives and works in San Francisco, United States, and in London, United Kingdom.

BALTHASAR BURKHARD
Born in 1944 in Berne, Switzerland. Lives and works in Berne and in Anduze, France.

POL BURY
Born in 1922 in Haine-Saint-Pierre, Belgique. Lives and works in Paris, France.

JEAN-MARC BUSTAMANTE*
Born in 1952 in Toulouse, France. Lives and works in Paris, France.

B

C

ANDRÉ CADERE*
Born in 1934 in Warsaw, Poland. Died in 1978 in Paris, France.

LOUIS CANE
Born in 1943 in Beaulieu-sur-Mer, France. Lives and works in Paris, France.

CÉSAR*
Born in 1921 in Marseille, France. Died in 1998 in Paris, France.

ALAN CHARLTON
Né en 1948 in Sheffield, United Kingdom. Lives and works in London, United Kingdom.

MARTIN BARRÉ
74-75-B-171X159, 1974-1975. ACRYLIC AND PENCIL ON CANVAS, 171 X 159 CM. PURCHASE, 1976

DANIEL BUREN
MANIFESTATION 1,1967. ACRYLIC ON FABRIC, 200 X 200 CM. PURCHASE, 1989

HANNE DARBOVEN
TEMPS DE L'ÉCRITURE : UNE VISION DU MONDE (SCHREIBZEIT : WELTANSICHTEN), 1975-1980. INK, COLLAGE, SILKSCREEN ON PAPER, 1400 FRAMED ELEMENTS, EACH ELEMENT: 41 X 29.5 CM. PURCHASE, 1992.

SIGMAR POLKE
MORSE (WALROSS), 1984.
OIL AND PIGMENTS ON CANVAS,
270 X 200 CM. PURCHASE, 1989.

LUCIANO FABRO
EUCLIDE, 1984. METAL,
300 X 300 X 300 CM.
PURCHASE, 1988.

GIOVANNI ANSELMO
TROIS CENTS MILLIONS D'ANNÉES
(TRECENTO MILLIONI DI ANNI), 1969.
ANTHRACITE, LAMP, CORRUGATED STEEL PLATE,
METAL WIRE, 30 X 56 X 25 CM. PURCHASE, 1986.

CHRISTO
Born in 1935 in Garovo, Bulgaria. Lives and works in New York, United States.

DAVID CLAERBOUT*
Born in 1969 in Courtrai, Belgium. Lives and works in Brussels, Belgium.

ALAIN CLÉMENT
Born in 1941 in Paris, France. Lives and works in Nimes, France.

CLAUDE CLOSKY
Born in 1963 in Paris, France. Lives and works in Paris, France.

JAMES COLEMAN*
Born in 1941 in Ballaghadrreen, Ireland. Lives and works in Dublin, Ireland.

GÉRARD COLLIN-THIÉBAUT
Born in 1946 in Lièpvre, France. Lives and works in Vuillafans, France.

ROBERT COMBAS*
Born in 1957 in Lyon, France. Lives and works in Paris, France.

TONY CRAGG*
Born in 1949 in Liverpool, United Kingdom. Lives and works in Wuppertal, Germany.

D

CUECO*
Born in 1929 in Uzerche, France. Lives and works in Paris, France.

JOSEF DABERNIG
Born in 1956 in Kötschach-Mauten, Austria. Lives and works in Vienna, Austria.

DADO
Born in 1933 in Cetinjie, Montenegro. Lives and works in Chaumont-en-Vexin, France.

HANNE DARBOVEN*
Born in 1941 in Munich, Germany. Lives and works in Hamburg, Germany.

TACITA DEAN*
Born in 1965 in Canterbury, United Kingdom. Lives and works in London, United Kingdom.

JEAN DEGOTTEX
Born in 1918 in Sathonay, France. Died in 1988 in Paris, France.

GÉRARD DESCHAMPS
Born in 1937 in Lyon, France. Lives and works in La Châtre, France.

MARC DEVADE
Born in 1943 in Paris, France. Died in 1983 in Paris, France.

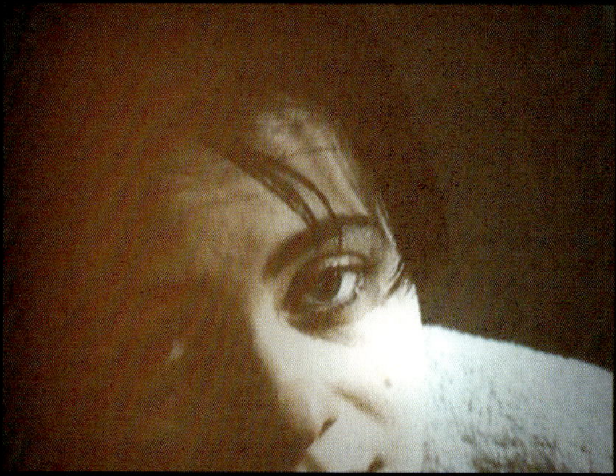

REBECCA BOURNIGAULT

SANS TITRE, 18 NOVEMBRE 1996 (DETAIL).
OVERHEAD CONTINUOUS PROJECTION OF VIDEO
AND SOUNDTRACK, COPY: 1/1. PURCHASE, 1998

TACITA DEAN

SOUND MIRRORS, 1999 (DETAIL). PROJECTION OF A 16MM FILM,
BLACK AND WHITE FILM, OPTICAL SOUND, LENGTH: 7', COPY: 3/4.
PURCHASE, 2001.

DAVID CLAERBOUT

VIETNAM 1967 - NEAR DUC PHO - RECONSTRUCTION AFTER HIROMISHI MINE, 2000

PETER FISCHLI ET DAVID WEISS

BÜSI, 2001 (DETAIL). CONTINOUS VIDEO LOOP PROJECTION, EDITION OF 150 COPIES, ARTISTS' PROOF. DONATED BY THE ARTISTS, 2002.

DOMINIQUE GONZALEZ-FOERSTER

CENTRAL, 2001 (DETAIL). AUDIO AND VIDEO PROJECTION OF A SUPER 8 FILM BLOWN UP TO 35 MM AND DIGITIZED, LENGTH: 10'30", COPY: 1/5. PURCHASE, 2002.

PIERRE HUYGHE

ATLANTIC (VERSIONS MULTIPLES GB/F/D), 1997 (DETAIL). SIMULTANEOUS VIDEOPROJECTION OF FRENCH, ENGLISH AND GERMAN VERSIONS OF THE EWALD ANDRE DUPONT FILM "ATLANTIC" (1929), COPY: 1/3. PURCHASE 1997.

DANIEL DEZEUZE*
Born in 1942 Alès, France.
Lives and works in Sète, France.

JAN DIBBETS*
Born in 1941 in Weert, Netherland. Lives and works in Amsterdam, Netherlands.

ERIK DIETMAN*
Born in 1937 in Jönkoping, Sweden.
Died in 2002 in Paris, France.

HERVÉ DI ROSA
Born in 1959 in Sète, France.
Lives and works in Sète, France.

TOM DRAHOS
Born in 1947 in Jablonne, Czech Republic. Lives and works in Paris, France.

FRANÇOIS DUFRÊNE
Born in 1930 in Paris, France.
Died in 1982 in Paris, France.

D

ERRÓ*
Born in 1932 in Olafsvik, Iceland. Lives and works in Paris, France.

E

ETIENNE-MARTIN
Born in 1913 in Coriol-sur-Drôme, France. Died in 1995 in Paris, France.

E

F

LUCIANO FABRO*
Born in 1936 in Turin, Italy.
Lives and works in Milan, Italy.

PATRICK FAIGENBAUM
Born in 1954 in Paris, France.
Lives and works in Paris, France.

BERNARD FAUCON
Born in 1950 in Apt, France.
Lives and works in Paris, France.

HANS-PETER FELDMANN*
Born in 1941 in Düsseldorf, Germany. Lives and works in Düsseldorf, Germany.

ROBERT FILLIOU
Born in 1926 in Sauve, France.
Died in 1987 in Les Eyzies-de-Tayac, France.

IAN HAMILTON FINLAY
Born in 1925 in Nassau, Bahamas.
Lives and works in Dunsyre Lanark, United Kingdom.

ROLAND FISCHER
Born in 1958 in Sarrebruck, Germany.
Lives and works in Munich, Germany.

PETER FISCHLI & DAVID WEISS*
Born in 1952 in Zurich, Switzerland.
Born in 1946 in Zurich. They live and work in Zurich, Switzerland.

ALAIN FLEISCHER
Born in 1944 in Paris, France.
Lives and works in Paris, France.

GLORIA FRIEDMANN*
Born in 1950 in Kronach, Germany.
Lives and works in Paris, France.

BERNARD FRIZE

REMOON, 2001. ACRYLIC AND RESIN ON CANVAS, 220 X 220 CM. PURCHASE, 2002.

HEAWOOD (DESSUS/DESSOUS), 1999. LACQUER ON FIBERGLASS, 140 X 84 X 23 CM EACH. PURCHASE, 2002

HENRI CUECO
MARX FREUD MAO,
1969–1970. OIL AND HIGH-GLOSS PAINT ON CANVAS, 162 X 130 CM. DONATED BY THE ARTIST, 2000.

ERRÓ
TROSKY, 1973.
HIGH-GLOSS PAINT ON CANVAS, 162 X 130 CM. PURCHASE, 2002.

GÉRARD FROMANGER
LA FRANCE EST-ELLE COUPÉE EN DEUX?, 1974. OIL ON CANVAS, 150 X 200 CM. PURCHASE, 1983.

JACQUES MONORY
TOXIQUE N°26, K. 1983. ACRYLIC ON PAPER MOUNTED ON CANVAS, WOOD, FABRIC, 150 X 230 CM. PURCHASE, 1984.

BERNARD RANCILLAC
DIANA ROSS, 1974. ACRYLIC ON CANVAS, 195 X 250 CM. PURCHASE, 1975.

GILBERT & GEORGE

CUNT, 1977. 16 FRAMED BLACK AND WHITE AND COLOR PHOTOGRAPHS, 241 X 201 CM. PURCHASE, 2000.

BERNARD FRIZE*
Born in 1945 in Saint-Mandé, France. Lives and works in Paris, France.

GÉRARD FROMANGER*
Born in 1939 à Jouars-Pontchartrain, France. Lives and works in Siena, Italy, and in Paris, France.

G

JEAN-LOUIS GARNELL
Born in 1954 in Dolo, France. Lives and works in Châtenay-Malabry, France.

GÉRARD GASIOROWSKI*
Born in 1930 in Paris, France. Died in 1986 in Lyon, France.

JOCHEN GERZ
Born in 1940 in Berlin, Germany. Lives and works in Paris, France.

PAUL-ARMAND GETTE*
Born in 1927 in Lyon, France. Lives and works in Paris, France.

GILBERT & GEORGE*
Gilbert Proersh, born in 1943 in the Dolomites, Italy. George Passmore, born in 1942 in the Devon, United Kingdom. Lives and works in London, United Kingdom.

DOMINIQUE GONZALEZ-FOERSTER*
Born in 1965 in Strasbourg, France. Lives and works in Paris, France.

ANDREAS GURSKY*
Born in 1955 in Leipzig, Germany. Lives and works in Düsseldorf, Germany.

H

HANS HAACKE
Born in 1936 in Cologne, Germany. Lives and works in New York, United States.

RAYMOND HAINS*
Born in 1926 in Saint-Brieuc, France. Lives and works in Nice and in Paris, France.

SIMON HANTAÏ*
Born in 1922 in Bia, Hungary. Lives and works in Paris, France.

KEITH HARING
Born in 1958 in Kunztown, United States. Died in 1990 in New York, United States.

GOTTFRIED HONEGER
Born in 1917 in Zurich, Suisse. Lives and works in Cannes, France.

RONI HORN
Born in 1955 in New York, États-Unis. Lives and works in New York.

CRAIGIE HORSFIELD
Born in 1949 in Cambridge, United Kingdom. Lives and works in London, United Kingdom.

ANDRÉ CADERE
PEINTURE SANS FIN/UNLIMITED PAINTING, 1972.
OIL ON WOODEN ROD, 210 CM, Ø 10 CM. PURCHASE, 1995.

SARKIS
BLACKOUT LEICA MUSEUM, 1976.
59 PANELS, PHOTOGRAPHS, PLEXIGLAS, EACH PANEL: 40 X 65 CM.
PURCHASE, 1989.

PAUL-ARMAND GETTE
LA PLAGE... ÉTÉ, 1973. 20 PANNELS CONTAINING BLACK
AND WHITE PHOTOGRAPHS, PHOTOSTATS, DOCUMENTS, LETRASET
ON BRISTOL BOARD, EACH PANEL: 70 X 50 CM. PURCHASE, 1992.

MARINE HUGONNIER
Born in 1969 in Paris, France. Lives and works in London, United Kingdom.

PIERRE HUYGHE*
Born in 1962 in Antony, France. Lives and works in New York, United States.

FABRICE HYBERT*
Born in 1961 in Luçon, France. Lives and works in Paris, France.

CHRISTIAN JACCARD
Born in 1939 in Fontenay-sous-Bois, France. Lives and works in Paris, France.

ALAIN JACQUET*
Born in 1939 in Neuilly-sur-Seine, France. Lives and works in Paris, France.

SHIRLEY JAFFE
Born in 1923 in Elizabeth, United States. Lives and works in Paris, France.

LOUIS JAMMES
Born in 1958 in Carcassonne, France. Lives and works in Paris, France.

GEORGES JEANCLOS
Born in 1933 in Paris, France. Died in 1997 in Paris, France.

BERNARD JOISTEN
Born in 1962 in Gap, France. Lives and works in Paris, France.

VALÉRIE JOUVE
Born in 1964 in Saint-Étienne, France. Lives and works in Paris, France.

GÜLSÜN KARAMUSTAFA
Born in 1946 en Turkey. Lives and works in Istanbul, Turkey.

SEYDOU KEITA
Born in 1912 in Bamako, Mali. Died in 2001 in Bamako, Mali.

JOËL KERMARREC
Born in 1939 in Ostende, Belgium. Lives and works in Paris, France.

PETER KLASEN*
Born in 1935 in Lübeck, Germany. Lives and works in Paris, France.

KAREN KNORR
Born 1954 in Francfort-sur-le-Main, Germany. Lives and works in London, United Kingdom.

MARIO MERZ
IGLOO FIBONACCI, 1970. METAL AND DRIED EARTH, NEON, 120 CM, Ø 160 CM. PURCHASE, 1987.

233
377
610
987

JOHN ARMLEDER
FURNITURE SCULPTURE 106, 1986.
FURNITURE (WOOD, 215X305X43CM),
PAINTINGS (ACRYLIC ON CANVAS,
167.6 X 109.2 CM AND 122 X 91.4 CM TWICE).
PURCHASE, 2001.

CLAUDE RUTAULT
DIPTYQUE, PROPOSITION N°41 DE
"DÉFINITIONS/MÉTHODES", 1973-1979.
PAINT ON CANVAS, 64.5 X 130 CM
AND 24.5 X 130 CM. PURCHASE, 1983.

OLIVIER MOSSET
(SANS TITRE), 1969.
OIL ON CANVAS,
100 X 100 CM. PURCHASE, 1989.

AURÉLIE NEMOURS
RYTHME DU MILLIMÈTRE SB 34,43,
1977. DIPTYCH, OIL ON CANVAS,
120 X 120 CM EACH PANEL. PURCHASE, 1984.

K

STANISLAS KOLIBAL
Born in 1925 in Orlova, Czech Republic. Lives and works in Prague, Czech Republic.

L

BERTRAND LAVIER*
Born in 1949 in Châtillon-sur-Seine, France. Lives and works in Paris and in Aignay-le-Duc, France.

ANGE LECCIA*
Born in 1952 in Morsiglia, France. Lives and works in Paris, France.

JEAN LE GAC
Born in 1936 in Alès, France. Lives and works in Paris, France.

JULIO LE PARC
Born in 1928 à Mendoza, Argentina. Lives and works in Antony, France.

CLAUDE LÉVÊQUE*
Born in 1953 in Nevers, France. Lives and works in Montreuil, France.

RICHARD LONG
Born in 1945 in Bristol, United Kingdom. Lives and works in Bristol, United Kingdom.

M

ROBERT MALAVAL
Born in 1937 in Nice, France. Died in 1980 in Paris, France.

MARIO MERZ*
Born in 1925 in Milan, Italy. Died in 2003 in Turin, Italy.

ANNETTE MESSAGER*
Born in 1943 in Berck, France. Lives and works in Malakoff, France.

JEAN-MICHEL MEURICE
Born in 1938 in Lille, France. Lives and works in Paris, France.

DUANE MICHALS
Born in 1932 in Mc Keesport, United States. Lives and works in New York, United States.

YANG PEI MING*
Born in 1960 in Shangai, China. Lives and works in Dijon, France.

JACQUES MONORY*
Born in 1934 in Paris, France. Lives and works in Cachan, France.

FRANÇOIS MORELLET
Born in 1926 in Cholet, France. Lives and works in Cholet, France.

ANNETTE MESSAGER
DOOOMESTIC, 2000. FABRIC, ROPE, 300 X 335 X 30 CM. PURCHASE, 2001.

JEAN-LUC MOULÈNE
S.T. (PONT D'IENA), 1994. COLOR PHOTOGRAPH, 120 X 150 CM. PURCHASE, 2000

JEAN-MARC BUSTAMANTE
T.11.78, 1978. COLOR PHOTOGRAPH,
103 X 130 CM. DONATED BY THE ARTIST, 2000.

OLIVIER MOSSET*
Born in 1944 in Berne, Switzerland. Lives and works in New York, United States.

CÔME MOSTA-HEIRT
Born in 1946 in Le Havre, France. Lives and works in Paris, France.

JEAN-LUC MOULÈNE*
Born in 1955 in Reims, France. Lives and works in Paris, France.

NICOLAS MOULIN*
Born in 1970 in Paris, France. Lives and works in Paris, France.

TANIA MOURAUD
Born in 1942 in Paris, France. Lives and works in Paris, France.

VALÉRIE MRÉJEN*
Born in 1969 in Paris, France. Lives and works in Paris, France.

JEAN-LUC MYLAYNE
Born in 1946 in Marquise, France. Lives and works in Ardres, France.

M

N

AURÉLIE NEMOURS*
Born in 1910 in Paris, France. Lives and works in Paris, France.

NILS-UDO
Born in 1937 in Lauf, Germany. Lives and works in Riedering, Germany.

N

O

DENNIS OPPENHEIM
Born in 1938 in Mason City, United States. Lives and works in New York, United States.

YVES OPPENHEIM
Born in 1948 in Madagascar. Lives and works in Paris, France.

GABRIEL OROZCO
Born in 1962 in Veracruz, Mexico. Lives and works in New York, United States.

JEAN-MICHEL OTHONIEL
Born in 1964 in Saint-Étienne, France. Lives and works in Paris, France.

O

P

NAM JUNE PAIK*
Born in 1932 in Seoul, South Korea. Lives and works in New York, United States.

PANAMARENKO*
Born in 1940 in Antwerp, Belgium. Lives and works in Antwerp, Belgium.

GERHARD RICHTER
ABSTRAKTES BILD (TABLEAU ABSTRAIT), 648-2, 1987. OIL ON CANVAS,
225 X 200 CM. PURCHASE, 1988.

ETTORE SPALLETTI
SUPERFICIE, 1990. PIGMENTS ON WOOD, 300X150CM. PURCHASE, 1994.
GRAND VASE (GRANDE VASO), 1990. PIGMENTS ON WOOD, 90 X 130 X 100 CM. PURCHASE, 1991.
SIGMAR POLKE
MORSE (WALROSS), 1984. OIL AND PIGMENTS ON CANVAS, 270 X 200 CM. PURCHASE, 1989.

JAN VERCRUYSSE

TOMBEAUX, 1991. MURANO BLOWN GLASS, STRIPS OF LEATHER, 566 X 650 CM. DONATED BY THE SOCIÉTÉ DES AMIS, 1992.

THOMAS SCHÜTTE

CITRONS NOIRS (SCHWARZE ZITRONEN), 1989. 20 ELEMENTS, BLACK ENAMELED CERAMIC, EACH PIECE: 69 X 41 CM OR 55 X 36 CM. PURCHASE, 1990.

DANIEL SPOERRI

DÉTROMPE L'ŒIL - FORÊT VIERGE, LA JUNGLE OU HOMMAGE AU DOUANIER ROUSSEAU,
1963. CARPET, VARIOUS OBJECTS ON CHIPBOARD, 120 X 172 X 100 CM. PURCHASE, 1995.

GUILIO PAOLINI
Born in 1940 in Genoa, Italy. Lives and works in Turin, Italy.

PHILIPPE PARRENO*
Born in 1964 in Oran, Algeria. Lives and works in Paris, France.

GIUSEPPE PENONE*
Born in 1947 in Garessio, Italy. Lives and works in San Raffaele Cimena, Italy.

ERNEST PIGNON-ERNEST
Born in 1942 in Nice, France. Lives and works in Paris, France.

JEAN-PIERRE PINCEMIN
Born in 1944 in Paris, France. Lives and works in Authon-la-Plaine, France.

ANNE ET PATRICK POIRIER
Born in 1942 in Marseille, France. Born in 1942 in Nantes, France. They live and work in Lourmarin, France.

ÉRIC POITEVIN
Born in 1961 in Longuyllon, France. Lives and works in Mangiennes, France.

SIGMAR POLKE*
Born in 1941 in Oels, Poland. Lives and works in Cologne, Germany.

P

R

BERNARD RANCILLAC*
Born in 1931 in Paris, France. Lives and works in Malakoff, France.

JEAN-PIERRE RAYNAUD*
Born in 1939 in Courbevoie, France. Lives and works in La Garenne-Colombes, France.

MARTIAL RAYSSE*
Born in 1936 à Vallauris, France. Lives and works in Issigeac, France.

PAUL REBEYROLLE
Born in 1926 in Eymoutier, France. Lives and works in Montigny-sur-Orge, France.

JUDIT REIGL*
Born inn 1923 in Kapuvar, Hungary. Lives and works in Marcoussis, France.

BERNARD RÉQUICHOT
Born in 1929 in Asnières-sur-Vègre, France. Died in 1961 à Paris, France.

GERHARD RICHTER*
Born in 1932 in Dresde, Germany. Lives and works in Cologne, Germany.

GUY DE ROUGEMONT
Born in 1935 in Paris, France. Lives and works in Paris, France.

MARINE HUGONNIER

ANNA HANUSOVA. 27.06.01,5 :40 , 2001 (DETAIL). AUDIOVISUAL INSTALLATION, AUDIO VIDEOPROJECTION, LENGTH: 10'17", COPY: 2/6. PURCHASE, 2002

VALÉRIE MRÉJEN

IL A FAIT BEAU, 1999 (DETAIL). VIDEO-AUDIO TRACK. PURCHASE, 2000.

PHILIPPE PARRENO

ANYWHERE OUT OF THE WORLD, 2000 (DETAIL). VIDEOPROJECTION, DIGITAL SOUND ANIMATION, LENGTH: 4’, COPY: 4/4. PURCHASE, 2001.

DOMINIQUE GONZALEZ-FOERSTER

ANN LEE IN ANZEN ZONE, 2000 (DETAIL). VIDEOPROJECTION, DIGITAL SOUND ANIMATION, LENGTH: 3’25”, COPY: 1/5. PURCHASE, 2001.

PIERRE HUYGHE

TWO MINUTES OUT OF TIME, 2000 (DETAIL). VIDEOPROJECTION, DIGITAL SOUND ANIMATION, LENGTH: 4’, COPY: 4/4. PURCHASE, 2001.

ANRİ SALA

İNTERVİSTA, 1998 (DETAIL). AUDIO VIDEOPROJECTION, LENGTH: 26', COPY: 1/6. PURCHASE, 2001.

FİONA TAN

PLUİE (RAİN), 2001 (DETAIL). SIMULTANEOUS BROADCAST OF TWO VIDEO TRACKS ON TWO MONITORS, COPY: 2/6. PURCHASE, 2001.

ROSEMARİE TROCKEL

JULİA-10-20 ANS, 1998 (DETAIL). VIDEO-AUDIO TRACK, LENGTH: 8', COPY: 4/10. PURCHASE, 2000.

GİLLİAN WEARİNG

TRAUMA, 2000 (DETAIL). VIDEO-AUDIO OVERHEAD VIDEO PROJECTION, LENGTH: 30', COPY: 2/5. PURCHASE, 2001.

R

S

CLAUDE RUTAULT*

Born in 1941 Les Trois-Moutiers, France. Lives and works in Vaucresson, France.

NIKI DE SAINT-PHALLE

Born in 1930 in Neuilly-sur-Seine, France. Died in 2002 in San Diego, United States.

ANRI SALA*

Born in 1974 in Tirana, Albania. Lives and works in Berlin, Germany.

JEAN-MICHEL SANEJOUAND

Born in 1934 in Lyon, France. Lives and works in Vaulandry, France.

SARKIS*

Born in 1938 in Istanbul, Turkey. Lives and works in Paris, France.

ANTONIO SEGUI

Born in 1934 in Cordoba, Argentina. Lives and works in Arcueil, France.

THOMAS SCHÜTTE*

Born in 1954 in Oldenburg, Germany. Lives and works in Düsseldorf, Germany.

THOMAS SHANNON

Born in 1947 in Los Angeles, United States. Lives and works in New York, United States.

ANNE-MARIE SCHNEIDER

Born in 1962 in Chauny, France. Lives and works in Paris, France.

JESUS RAFAEL SOTO

Born in 1923 in Ciudad Bolivar, Venezuela. Lives and works in Paris, France.

PIERRE SOULAGES*

Born in 1919 in Rodez, France. Lives and works in Paris and Sète, France.

ETTORE SPALLETTI*

Born in 1940 in Capelle Sul Tavo, Italy. Lives and works in Pescara, Italy.

DANIEL SPOERRI*

Born in 1930 in Galatzi, Rumania. Lives and works in Ferrières, France.

GEORGES TONY STOLL

Born in 1955 in Marseille, France. Lives and works in Paris, France.

NIELE TORONI

CABINET DE PEINTURE, 1989. MARKS OF BRUSH N°50 REPEATED AT REGULAR INTERVALS OF 30 CM, ACRYLIC PAINT ON WALL AND ON TRACING PAPER. COMMISSIONED FROM THE ARTIST, 1989.

CLAUDE VIALLAT
SANS TITRE N°3, 1968. DYE ON RAW CANVAS, 310 X 286 CM. PURCHASE, 2001.

DANIEL DEZEUZE
SANS TITRE, 1975. STRIPS OF PAINTED, STAPLED WOOD, 590 X 135 CM. PURCHASE, 1990.

GÉRARD FROMANGER
ROUGE 1, 1968 (DETAIL). DVD FILM.
DONATED BY THE ARTIST, 2001.

CLAUDE VIALLAT
FILET POLYCHROME, 1970-1971. COLORED ROPES,
280 X 240 CM. PURCHASE, 1974.

BEAT STREULI
Born in 1957 in Altdorf, Switzerland. Lives and works in Dusseldorf, Germany.

TAKIS
Born in 1925 in Athens, Greece. Lives and works in Paris, France.

FIONA TAN*
Born in 1966 in Indonesia. Lives and works in Amsterdam, Netherlands.

VIBEKE TANDBERG
Born in 1967 in Oslo, Norway. Lives and works in Oslo, Norway, and in New York, United States.

HERVÉ TÉLÉMAQUE*
Born in 1937 in Port-au-Prince, Haiti. Lives and works in Villejuif, France.

JEAN TINGUELY
Born in 1925 in Fribourg, Switzerland. Died in 1991 in Bern, Switzerland.

GÉRARD TITUS-CARMEL
Born in 1942 in Paris, France. Lives and works in Oulchy-le-Château, France.

NIELE TORONI*
Born in 1937 in Locarno-Muralto, Switzerland. Lives and works in Paris, France.

PATRICK TOSANI*
Born in 1954 in Boissy-L'Aillerie, France. Lives and works in Paris, France.

DANIEL TREMBLAY
Born in 1950 in Angers, France. Died in 1985 in Angers, France.

ROSEMARIE TROCKEL*
Born in 1952 in Schwerte, Germany. Lives and works in Cologne, Germany.

VICTOR VASARELY
Born in 1908 in Pécs, Hungary. Died in 1997 in Paris, France.

FELICE VARINI*
Born in 1952 in Locarno, Switzerland. Lives and works in Paris, France.

VLADIMIR VELICKOVIC
Born in 1935 in Belgrade, Serbia. Lives and works in Paris, France.

FELICE VARINI
273 BD PEREIRE, PARIS, 1989. ACRYLIC, VARIABLE DIMENSIONS. PURCHASE, 1997.

JAN VERCRUYSSE*
Born in 1948 in Waregen, Belgium. Lives and works in Brussels, Belgium.

FRANÇOISE VERGIER
Born in 1952 in Grignan, France. Lives and works in Paris and in Grignan, France.

MICHEL VERJUX
Boen in 1956 in Chalon-sur-Saône, France. Lives and works in Paris, France.

CLAUDE VIALLAT*
Born in 1936 in Nimes, France. Lives and works in Nimes, France.

JACQUES VILLEGLÉ*
Born in 1925 in Quimper, France. Lives and works in Paris, France.

WOLF VOSTELL
Born in 1932 in Leverkusen, Germany. Died in 1998 in Berlin, Germany.

V

W

GILLIAN WEARING*
Born in 1963 in Birmingham, United Kingdom. Lives and works in London, United Kingdom.

LAWRENCE WEINER
Born in 1942 in New York, United States. Lives and works in New York and in Amsterdam, Netherlands.

MARTHE WERY
Born in 1930 in Brussels, Belgium. Died in 2005 in Brussels, Belgium.

ZAO WOU-KI*
Born in 1921 in Beijing, China. Lives and works in Paris, France.

W

Y

YVARAL
Born in 1934 in Paris, France. Died in 2002 in Paris, France.

Y

RÉMY ZAUGG*
Born in 1943 in Courgenay, Switzerland. Lives and works in Basel, Switzerland.

Z

MICHELE ZAZA
Born in Molfetta, Italy. Lives and works in Molfetta, Italy.

Z

MICHELE ZAZA
TEMPO TERRESTRE, 1978. SERIES OF 10 COLOR PHOTOGRAPHS. EACH ONE: 29.5 X 39.5 CM. PURCHASE, 1982.
RICHARD LONG
LA LIGNE DE SAINT-JUST (SAINT-JUST LINE), 1986. RED SCHIST, 900 X 100 CM. PURCHASE, 1986.

USEFUL INFORMATION

ENTRANCE

11, avenue du Président-Wilson 75116 Paris
Tel: 01 53 67 40 00.

OPENING HOURS

Permanent collection
and temporary exhibitions: Tuesday to Sunday
Closed Monday and public holidays.

ACCESS

Métro Alma-Marceau ou Iéna
RER: Pont de l'Alma (line C)
Bus n°s 32, 42, 63, 72, 80, 92

www.mam.paris.fr

Prior reservations required for groups: 01 53 67 40 80.

GRAPHIC DESIGN
FBI (Béatrice C. Bodin, Yan Stive)
EDITORS
Isabelle Gilloots, Cécile Guibert, Joseph Jacquet
TRANSLATION
Lisa Davidson
PRODUCTION
Audrey Chenu, Alice Piton, Vincent Benzi
PHOTO RESEARCH AND PATRIMONIAL RIGHTS
Laurence Goupille, Viviane Linois
COLOR SEPARATION
Fotimprim, Paris
PRINTING
Snoeck-Ducaju & Zoon, Ghent, Belgium

Printed by Snoeck-Ducaju & Zoon in Ghent, Belgium, June 2005

The text of this book was set in Letter Gothic, FBI created an original typeface for the titles.
Paper: Gardamat 135 g

ISBN 2-87900-866-2 - AS 1305
Dépôt légal: June 2005
Diffusion Actes Sud - Distribution UD-Union Distribution

PHOTOGRAPHIC CREDITS (The numbers refer to page numbers)

Baranger © Archives Photo. Paris / CMN: 19, 22, 23, 25 ■ © Paris, Musées / Karin Maucotel: 150-151, 154-155, 160-161, 172-173, 176-177, 180-181, 184 (bottom), 186, 191 (left), 200 (right), 208-209, 212-213, 215, 225, 226-227, 230-231, 233, 234-235, 239, 242-243, 247 (top), 252-253, 254, 257 ■ © Christophe Walter: 166-167 ■ © Pierre Huyghe / Galerie Marian Goodman, Paris: 222-223 (bottom) 247 (right bottom) ■ © André Morin: 216, 217 ■ © Photothèque des musées de la ville de Paris: 57, 82, 141 (bottom); Rémi Briant: 77, 79 (top), 85 (bottom), 86 (top), 90; Chevallier: 45 (top), 72, 98, 114, 123, 125; Charles Delepelaire: 42, 45 (bottom), 46, 50, 54, 55, 60, 63, 80, 89, 93, 96, 104, 108, 121, 126, 129, 137, 142, 165, 188 (left), 189 (right), 199 (right); Dubroca: 97; Philippe Joffre: 14, 31, 37, 38, 40, 41, 49, 52, 53, 58, 59, 64, 67, 70, 85 (top), 86 (bottom), 92, 101, 103, 105, 106, 107, 111, 117, 118, 128, 132, 138, 145, 168, 183, 185, 192 (right), 194, 195 (right), 196 (top), 200 (left), 202, 204-205, 210, 228, 236, 238; Philippe Joffre, Lyliane Degrâces: 76, 197, 244, 249 (top); Philippe Ladet: 134, 184 (top), 188 (right), 190 (right), 192 (left), 203 (right), 207, 220 (bottom), 221, 223 (top), 246 (top), 247 (bottom left), 248, 249 (bottom); Philippe Ladet, Lyliane Degrâces: 201 (right); Patrick Pierrain: 73, 113, 163, 193, 195 (left); Jean-Yves Trocaz: 75, 83, 95, 135, 141 (top), 189 (left), 191 (right), 199 (left), 201 (left), 203 (left), 241

RIGHTS RESERVED

79 (bottom), 190 (left), 196 (bottom), 198, 218, 220 (top), 222, 246 (bottom), 251

PATRIMONIAL RIGHTS

© ADAGP, Paris 2003: M. Abakanowicz, V. Adami, G. Aillaud, J.-M. Alberola, Arman, J. Arp, E. Ballet, M. Barré, J.-P. Bertrand, C. Boltanski, P. Bonnard, L. Bourgeois, G. Braque, V. Brauner, P. Buraglio, D. Buren, J.-M. Bustamante, A. Cadere, César, M. Chagall, G. Chaissac, G. de Chirico, R. Combas, J. Crotti, H. Cueco, A. Derain, D. Dezeuze, J. Dibbets, E. Dietman, J. Dubuffet, R. Dufy, M. Ernst, Erró, J. Fautrier, H.-P. Feldmann, L. Foujita, G. Friedmann, P.-A. Gette, A. Gleizes, D. Gonzalez-Foerster, M. Gromaire, A. Gursky, R. Hains, H. Hartung, J. Hélion, A. Herbin, F. Hybert, A. Jacquet, P. Klasen, F. Kupka, H. Laurens, B. Lavier, A. Leccia, F. Léger, E. Leroy, C. Lévêque, A. Lhote, A. Masson, A. Messager, J. Metzinger, J. Monory, A. Nemours, A. Ozenfant, J. Pascin, G. Penone, F. Picabia, B. Rancillac, J.-P. Raynaud, M. Raysse, G. Rouault, Sarkis, T. Schütte, K. Schwitters, P. Soulages, C. Soutine, D. Spoerri, H. Télémaque, J. Torres-García, P. Tosani, R. Trockel, K. Van Dongen, F. Varini, J. Vercruysse, C. Viallat, J. Villeglé, É. Vuillard, O. Zadkine, W.-K. Zao ■ © ADAGP, Paris 2004: H. Bellmer, P. Buraglio, J.-M. Bustamante, V. Brauner, D. Gonzalez-Foerster, J.-L. Moulène, F. Picabia, J. Reigl, R. Ubac, M. de Vlaminck ■ © Succession Marcel Duchamp - Adagp, Paris 2004 ■ © Man Ray Trust - Adagp, Paris 2004 ■ © Absalon (Eshel Meir, known as) / Courtesy galerie Étienne Ficheroulle ■ © Estate Brassaï / R.M.N. Claude Cahun © Zabriskie Gallery, United States ■ © 2004 David Claerbout / SOFAM, Belgium R. Delaunay & S. Delaunay © L&M Services B.V. Amsterdam 20030406 ■ © Fondazione Lucio Fontana, Milan ■ © Gérard Gasiorowski / Courtesy Galerie Maeght, Paris ■ Pierre Huyghe © Marian Goodman Gallery Paris / New York ■ Pierre Jahan © Olivier Lacroix ■ © Succession H. Matisse ■ © Nicolas Moulin / Courtesy Galerie chez Valentin, Paris ■ © Valérie Mréjen / Courtesy Galerie cent 8 ■ © Succession Picasso 2003 ■ © Anri Sala / Idéale Audience International, Galerie Chantal Crousel, Paris ■ © Gillian Wearing, courtesy Maureen Paley Interim Art, London ■ Rémy Zaugg © Fondation Rémy et Michèle Zaugg, Basel ■ © G. Anselmo, J. Armleder, G. Baselitz, B. & H. Becher, R. Bournigault, H. Brandl, J. Coleman, T. Cragg, H. Darboven, T. Dean, L. Fabro, P. Fischli & D. Weiss, B. Frize, G. Fromanger, Gilbert & George, B. Gysin, S. Hantaï, M. Hugonnier, R. Long, M. Merz, Y. P. Ming, O. Mosset, N. J. Paik, Panamarenko, P. Parreno, S. Polke, G. Richter, C. Rutault, E. Spalletti, F. Tan, N. Toroni, M. Zaza ■ Rights reserved: © B. Gysin